MW00826384

Celebrate ELVIS

Private Conversations • Never Before Published Interviews • Rumor Busters • Elvis Trivia & Facts • Q&A with Joe

A TCB JOE PUBLISHING PAPERBACK

Celebrate**ELVIS**

Published by TCB Joe Publishing

A division of TCB Joe Enterprises, LLC

Book & Cover Design by Lauren McMullen and The Dream Factory

TCB Joe books may be purchased for
business or promotional use or for special sales.
For more information please write to: info@tcbjoepublishing.com

ISBN: 0-9778945-3-3

Welcome to Celebrate Elvis, the book series that pays tribute to and facilitates a deeper understanding and appreciation of the world's most celebrated entertainer, my friend, Elvis Presley.

In this volume, we'll go back and relive the fun times at the Circle G Ranch. We'll visit upstairs at Graceland and spend some time remembering Elvis in the recording studio. We'll also take a look at the Army cover-up rumor and share some highly entertaining fan interviews. All this and much more in this volume of Celebrate Elvis...

This volume is dedicated to Charlie Hodge.

--Joe Esposito

Our deepest gratitude goes out to:

A.J.	Fay Freeman	Monica Pizano
Karlos Alvarez	Veronica Heeres	Jacqueline Raphael
Jeff Aron	Charlotte Hendry	Stephane Roussel
Michael Anderson	Maria Hesterberg	Ruth Sheppard
Wendy Bishop	Tally Lauriti	Stephen Skrypnyk
Jeffro Blues	Henry Lee	Yvonne Smith
Charles Boyer	Linda Mackenzie	Gaylon Spencer
Ashley Brooks	Luke Mayama	Richard Stables
Danielle Cantrell	Rhonda McKinney	Dawn Stedman
David Cammack	Michael McLeavy	Andie Stoeckle
John Campolo	David Morgan	Alan Thompson
Adela Caputo	Terry Muise	Shirley Toffling
Ricky Cole	Eric Murray	Frank Valente
Jimmy Diele	Danielle Offord	Dianna Weisner
Brian Flynn	Juanita Pasquini	Gina Wilson

What Really Happened?

Interview Excerpt with Joe Esposito

Reporter: It has been said that shortly before Elvis was to be discharged from the Army, he showed signs of reluctance to return to the United States for a variety of reasons, particularly since his mother was no longer around. Could you describe the atmosphere around Elvis the last few days you spent with him in Germany before he left?

Joe Esposito: Well, I don't know where that story came from. Elvis was thrilled to be going back home. He wanted to get back to Memphis, see his friends and family and get back to Graceland. Sure, I know that inside of his heart, he was probably saying, "Well, my mom's not there anymore," and that sort of thing. Elvis didn't talk about it. You see, Elvis didn't talk about those things too much. He wasn't that type of guy. He usually kept everything inside of him. He loved his mother so much. He was definitely thinking about her not being there, but he never talked to me about it. Let's put it that way. He was just thrilled to be going back home to the United States. ♦

Did You Know?

Elvis bulldozed Billy Smith's house behind Graceland in order to enlarge the riding area. ♦

■**TRIVIA QUESTION** / View answer on next page

Who were some of the actors Elvis studied and loved watching on the big screen before heading off to Hollywood? Please name the 3 he most wanted to emulate.

Up Close and Personal:
The Circle G Ranch

A candid conversation between Joe Esposito and Daniel Lombardy

Daniel: Circle G Ranch, what do you remember about those times?

Joe: Well, that was another thing Elvis did. Remember, he never did anything in small ways. He decided to go buy a horse for Priscilla one Christmas. So naturally, he had to buy a second one for someone to ride with Priscilla so she didn't have to ride by herself. So he bought one for Jerry Schilling's wife, Sandy. After he buys the horses for both of them, he decides to get a horse for himself, after seeing both of them just having a ball and having so much fun riding around Graceland together. So he said, "Uh, I need a horse now." So he gets his horse. Then he gets a horse for Jerry Schilling. Then he really caught fire and bought one for everybody!

He tried to buy me one, but I said, "Elvis, I like Westerns and all, but I'm not an Italian John Wayne. Besides, I don't even know how to ride a horse."

That's funny. I could not imagine you pretending to be John Wayne saying, "Hey, Elvis, is that a horse I see before me?"

Hardly. As Elvis kept buying the horses, he started running out of stable space at Graceland. So instead of sheltering them in the main house or in the open, he decided to look for a ranch. So he goes over to Mississippi with Alan Fortas and Priscilla. They're driving around

---

■ **TRIVIA ANSWER** / Answer to question on previous page
James Dean, Marlon Brando, Yul Brynner

and came across this great little house for sale. They both looked at it and loved it right away. It came with 160 acres and was absolutely gorgeous. It was like a big golf course with a 4-acre lake that had what appeared to be a 20-foot high cross in the middle of it that had lights shining on it at night.

Wow! Most people only have about an acre of grass on their property these days, just big enough for a ground hog to nest there without getting a hunchback.

I know. I know. So this lake had this big bridge that went across to the other side. It was a nice bridge that also came with night lights so you could walk across anytime you wanted.

So Elvis decides to buy this property right off the bat without trying to cut the price down. He just bought it.

Now when Elvis is really into something, he goes absolutely crazy! He gets into his new role. He is enthusiastic and all motivated. He says, "Well, now you guys gotta live on the ranch with us." I said, "Well, Elvis, there's only a little house there that will comfortably house only you and Priscilla. You want us sleeping on the floor or in the closets standing up?"

Seriously, Daniel, that house was not that big. I sometimes had the feeling that we would knock out the window if we put the key in the lock too hard.

■ **TRIVIA QUESTION** / View answer on next page
What type of movies did Elvis really get into?

So Elvis came back with, "I'm buying trailers for everybody." He goes and buys a bunch of trailers for all of us and puts them way in the back of the ranch. It was a beautiful area, a really great area.

At the time, Elvis was between movies. We would go out there and just hang out every day. Elvis would ride his horse all over the place, all day long. He would often ride up to your trailer and knock on the door. There he was with his cowboy hat on, his cowboy boots, his chaps and his leather jacket. Elvis became a cowboy all of a sudden. It was great! Those times were a lot of fun. We used to have barbecues in the evenings and eat at long tables. Sometimes I would cook, and sometimes some of the other guys would cook. It was just such a great time. We also used to do skeet shooting over the lake. That was a lot of fun. So he did that routine over and over again. Then, little by little, the overkilling thing started where he did something so much that he simply got bored and tired with it. That was that, which of course meant the end to the Circle G Ranch.

That sounds like it was a lot of fun there.

Oh, it was just fabulous. I have quite a few home movies from that and all the stuff from Hawaii that really showed everybody having a great time. ♦

Did You Know?

Colonel Parker at one time conceived of the idea for a pay-per-view closed-circuit theatrical showing of a special Elvis concert in 1970. ♦

■ **TRIVIA ANSWER** / Answer to question on previous page
He loved English humor. Monty Python, movies with Peter Sellers, etc.

What Really Happened?

Interview Excerpt with Joe Esposito

Reporter: Mr. Esposito, it was written somewhere by people closest to Elvis that he suffered a perforated eardrum while being around big cannons at Fort Hood. The Army took notice and quickly pulled Elvis out of tanks and directly into the scouts. Is this really how Elvis became a scout driver?

Joe Esposito: Ah, that story is not true at all. He did not have a perforated ear. He never did, ok. His ears were hurting every time the tank barrels would discharge a round. I'll put it that way. It was just way too loud for him and it was physically hurting his ears. The word probably got back to one of the sergeants in charge, and he in turn probably recommended that they make him a scout to preserve his hearing since he was a world-class entertainer.

I think it's time to explain what happens when a person has a perforated eardrum to once and for all put this rumor in the trash were it belongs. According to medical doctors, the symptoms for ear perforation are among other things: moderate to severe imbalance, ringing in the ears, loss of hearing joined by chronic headaches so severe you wouldn't care if the local pet shop cut your hair. So my question about this rumor is this. If the rumor were true, then why did we not see Elvis suffering from any of these symptoms while he was giving the famous departure TV interview going to Germany? Better yet, would

---

■ **TRIVIA QUESTION** / View answer on next page

Who was the legendary Hall of Famer who interviewed Elvis when he was playing in Canada in 1957?

we have seen Elvis carrying his duffle bag on his shoulder down the walkway without assistance? He was supposed to be suffering from imbalance, remember? Since we are on a roll let's not forget seeing Elvis cheerfully singing in the shower while water was pounding into his ears in a scene from G.I. BLUES shortly after he left the service. I think that if the perforated ear nonsense were true, we more than likely would have seen Elvis in the shower with a Space helmet. ♦

Ask Joe

I have a letter here from Alan Thompson.

Alan says:

Being a huge fan of both Elvis Presley and Triumph motorcycle, I wonder if Elvis ever owned this brand of motorcycle? I know he bought several of them in Los Angeles in the 60's for the guys while he rode his Harley. I would like to know if he liked Triumphs for himself?

Alan, all I ever saw him ride was a Harley. Yes, he did buy the guys Triumph motorcycles. Elvis, on the other hand, always loved Harleys. We would ride all around town on Triumphs with Elvis being the leader on his Harley. That's just the way it was. He loved motorcycles as we all know. We had a great time riding them. Then, after awhile, a few of the guys started getting into accidents and got really hurt. So we stopped riding them. Thank God Elvis never got into an accident with his bike! That could have been bad. ♦

What Really Happened?

Interview Excerpt with Joe Esposito

Reporter: Joe, it was said that while Elvis was in Germany, he listened to a lot of European music, especially Mario Lanza, which was a major influence on him recording his version of "O Sole Mio," which he re-titled "It's Now Or Never." Do you know if Elvis was heading into the crooner direction with his music as RCA stated in an interview while Elvis was still in the Army?

Joe Esposito: Elvis listened to a lot of music while he was in the service. He wasn't just listening to Mario Lanza because he was over there. Elvis always listened to Mario Lanza. He listened to a variety of opera singers. He loved people with great voices. As far as *O Sole Mio, It's Now Or Never,* or *Surrender,* all of those were strong Italian songs. He really enjoyed singing powerful songs like that because he could use that great voice of his. He also really loved meaningful ballads. He would rather sing those instead of just playing ole rock 'n' roll, you know, *Tutti Frutti* and stuff like that. You saw a big difference in him when he sang the ballads, but he always listened to opera, gospel, or country, basically everything really and not just one style while he was in Europe.

So the statement RCA made about Elvis heading into the crooner direction with his music when he got back to the States was not correct?

Well, I don't know where RCA came up with that idea. There's no truth to that whatsoever. Someone I guess in the PR department decided to throw that out there. No, he was never going to change his style. ♦

■ **TRIVIA QUESTION** / View answer on next page

Who made up the Million Dollar Quartet?

Fan Spotlight Interview

With Ruth Sheppard

My name is Ruth Sheppard, and I reside in Silver Spring, Maryland. I love Elvis. I mean, he's my favorite artist. I always had a mad crush on him. My bedroom was covered in Elvis when I was a teenager. That means I'm old [laughing].

Daniel Lombardy: [laughing] No it doesn't. Old is a state of mind. Right?

Ok, that's true.

Ruth, what would you consider some of your favorite Elvis movies and songs?

Oh my gosh! My favorite Elvis song is actually *Love Me Tender* believe it or not and *The Wonder Of You*. Those are my favorites. As for my favorite movies, sounds corny, but LOVE ME TENDER.

Love me tender,
love me sweet,
never let me go.
You have made
my life complete,
and I love you so.
Love me tender,

Art provided by The Dream Factory from the upcoming book ELVIS IN ART

■ **TRIVIA ANSWER** / Answer to question on previous page
Johnny Cash, Jerry Lee Lewis, Carl Perkins and of course, Elvis.

Well, it's not corny! It's a great movie.

I mean, I thought he was a great artist in his first movie.

Ruth, what would you tell Joe Esposito if you were on the phone with him right now?

How the hell are you [laughing]?

[Laughing]

Joe, when are you coming to Baltimore? You haven't seen my Elvis house yet. So you still have to come here. We bought the house next door, and it's all made up in Elvis. We figured everybody else has an Elvis room. We had to outdo them!

That's right. You had to create your very own Elvis land.

That's right [laughing].

That's one way to win the battle of the Jones's isn't it?

Sure is [laughing]!

Ruth, what would you like to tell the other Elvis fans out there?

Regarding Elvis or Joe?

Elvis

The first thing that comes to mind is that Elvis was very funny and that he was wonderful. He was a good person, a very good person. ♦

■ **TRIVIA QUESTION** / View answer on next page

Who was the person that introduced Elvis when he performed on the famous flatbed truck that served as a stage in Memphis?

Always On My Mind

Hi, my name is Michael Anderson, and I'm living in Sweden in Gothenburg. I'm an Elvis fan. Elvis just exploded in my head when I heard Elvis, when he did the ALOHA FROM HAWAII concert. When I saw it on the TV in Sweden, it just blew my mind away. Since that night, I play Elvis everyday. He means everything for me. Because I have the love for Elvis, I met my girlfriend last year in January in Memphis. She's from Sweden too. We have been by coincidence living in the same town. So thanks to Elvis, I have a very beautiful girlfriend today. He is everything for me. ♦

Did You Know?

Elvis circled over Circle G Ranch with a Lear jet while on route to Memphis from a Nashville recording session. ♦

Always On My Mind

My name is Charlotte Hendry, and I reside in Monterey, California. Elvis has affected my life in many ways since I was a small child. He was caring, giving, loving. He's everything to me. When I am down, nothing, and I mean nothing, helps me cope better than listening to Elvis from his music to his movies. It's just everything that he does, everything he's about. ♦

■ **TRIVIA ANSWER** / Answer to question on previous page
George Klein

What Really Happened?

Interview Excerpt with Joe Esposito

Reporter: *Is it true that just because Colonel kept Elvis from entertaining the troops, it didn't mean he never sang any music in Germany? I have heard that he, indeed, did play at the night clubs like the Moulin Rouge in Munich or the Lido in Paris. Can you shed some light on this?*

Joe Esposito: When Elvis was in the service, he made up his mind that he was not going to do any performing and that's what happened. He did not perform.

As for the rumors about Elvis performing at the Moulin Rouge or some of the clubs in Paris, it never happened. So what was said about his performing in Europe is not true at all. The only time you would hear Elvis sing in Germany was at his house in Bad Nauheim, sitting at the piano in the evenings after work.

We would typically just hang out and talk and have a great time and everything, but as far as public performances, they never happened. The only time I ever saw him sing on a stage in Germany was when he had his birthday party held at a rented Special Forces hall on January 8, 1960, before leaving the service. We had all the guys there along with Priscilla. During the birthday party Elvis did sing a few songs, but it was just for us. He was up there with his guitar, and that was it. So outside of this private party, he never did any performing on stage during the time he was in the Army whatsoever. ◆

■ **TRIVIA QUESTION** / View answer on next page

Who was the first DJ to play an Elvis record on the radio; and who was it that encouraged him to play it?

What Really Happened?

Interview Excerpt with Joe Esposito

Reporter: It has been written that Elvis admired Charles Boyer recitations during songs. What memories does this bring back for you?

Joe Esposito: Somebody played this one song, *Softly As I Leave You,* by Charles Boyer. We played it over and over and over again. Practically wore it out! Elvis loved this one song by Charles Boyer so much that he copied the entire album and had a bunch of records made for personal use. Back then, tape recorders were not around yet. So he gave all of his friends and people he liked a copy of it. It was just a wonderful song. Like I said in previous interviews, when Elvis got onto something, man you heard it over and over and over again. We played it all the damn time. Practically wore that song out. It really was a great song.

What about "Green, Green, Grass Of Home?" I heard that you had a similar experience with that song driving back to Memphis while listening to it.

That's exactly right. We just completed a movie and were driving back to Memphis on the bus. Once we got within range of Memphis, we started receiving WHBQ where our friend, George Klein, was a disc jockey. It just so happens, that once we got in range, we picked up George on the radio and he was playing Tom Jones's *Green, Green, Grass Of Home.* So we heard it, and back in those days you didn't have

---

■ **TRIVIA ANSWER** / Answer to question on previous page
Dewey Phillips, Sam Phillips

cell phones like you do today. So Elvis says, "We have to hear that song again." So we stop at the next service station, get on the phone and call George at the radio station. "George, Elvis wants to hear it a few more times. Let's play it again for him, will ya?" So we get back on the bus and heard George announce, "I just got off the phone with a bunch of my friends driving back from California and they want to hear Tom Jones's version of *Green, Green, Grass Of Home*." He wound up playing it about 6 or 7 times. People were calling the station and asking, "Why do you keep playing that damn song over and over again?" And George said, "Because Elvis wants to hear it." So they would say, "Oh! Ok, no problem." ♦

What Really Happened?

Interview Excerpt with Joe Esposito

Reporter: Before the Timex-sponsored FRANK SINATRA SHOW - WELCOME HOME ELVIS aired, you guys traveled to Florida by train and got off on the outskirts of Miami. What was the reason for this?

Joe Esposito: That did not happen in Miami. That happened in Los Angeles. The home video footage you sometimes see of Elvis arriving by train and getting into a car was actually shot on the outskirts of Los Angeles. The reason Colonel did this was to hush Elvis's arrival into Los Angeles a little. We got off the train and rode into Los Angeles in cars. That's what happened. ♦

■ **TRIVIA QUESTION** / View answer on next page

Who shared Elvis's quarters on the ship while he was heading to Germany?

Ask Joe

I have a letter here from Brian Flynn.

Brian says:

Hi Joe, could you please tell me if Elvis could really play the guitar, or as he said onstage once, that he only knew four chords? Did he play any other instruments?

Oh! That's true, Brian. Elvis was never a great guitar player. He did play chords. Since I'm not a musician, I don't know all of the technical aspects of playing a guitar to tell you the truth. The amazing thing about Elvis was that he could sometimes pick up an instrument and have a knack for it. He oftentimes just sat down at the piano and played it really well. Or at other times, he would just pick up either a banjo or a violin, fiddle around with it and get some decent sound coming out. Like I said, he would play around with them a little. He was really good that way. I would say the piano was the best instrument I've seen him play. He would play that a lot. ♦

Fan Spotlight Interview

With Jimmy Diele

My name is Jimmy Diele, and I'm from Brooklyn, New York.

I loved Elvis since I was a little kid. A neighbor who was a gigantic Elvis fan introduced me to him. I fell in love with his music and style. My life has never been the same. I have made it a ritual to go to Graceland often. It's just a huge part of my life.

■ **TRIVIA ANSWER** / Answer to question on previous page
  Charlie Hodge, (may you rest in peace my friend)

Daniel Lombardy: Jimmy, what are some of the Elvis movies you enjoy watching along with some of the Elvis songs you enjoy listening to?

Oh! That has got to be VIVA LAS VEGAS. I just love that movie with Ann Margret and SPEEDWAY with Nancy Sinatra. They are both fantastic movies with some incredibly pretty ladies in them.

How right you are, Jimmy. You are probably very modest about that, right?

That's for sure [laughing]!

What about some of your favorite Elvis songs?

Elvis songs, I like them all. I mean, of course, I have some favorites like *Teddy Bear* and *Suspicious Minds*.

I also get into the more rare stuff you don't hear so much, but what I

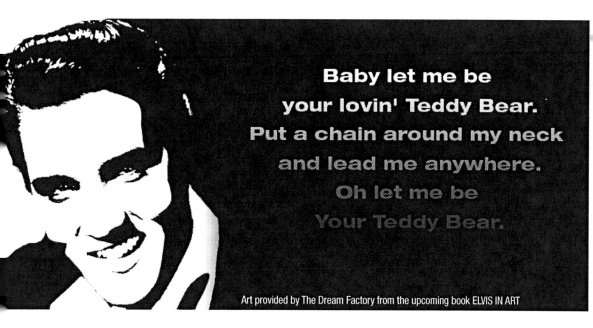

Baby let me be
your lovin' Teddy Bear.
Put a chain around my neck
and lead me anywhere.
Oh let me be
Your Teddy Bear.

Art provided by The Dream Factory from the upcoming book ELVIS IN ART

■ **TRIVIA QUESTION** / View answer on next page
Who was the beat behind Elvis from '55 to '68?

really love are the outtakes on some of the recording sessions. You just don't know what Elvis is going to do or what he is going to say next. It's just great what you can pick up from some of those conversations he has with the sound engineers. Love that stuff.

What are some of the things you would tell Joe if you were speaking with him right now?

I would say, "Joe, you're the best! You had Elvis as a personal friend, and you keep everybody straight about the facts on Elvis. I really respect the way you keep on taking care of business for your friend on and off camera. It is very inspiring to see you do that. I wish there would have been more people like you around Elvis while he was still alive. I am sure others would agree with me that you stuck with him no matter how difficult things got. You did the right thing, even when some of those other guys didn't do the right thing."

How would we personally feel if people we briefly knew in high school were still going around saying bad things about us once we are grown up, married with kids years later? Just because Elvis was a public figure and you worked, played and lived with him doesn't mean that you can just take him apart after he passes away. Elvis is not just some guy off the street that they are bad mouthing. You know? Anyone that was around Elvis has to realize that this remarkable man and his music heavily connected to and still influences the fans. They need to be responsible. The stuff they say has tremendous consequences that affect the younger generation of Elvis fans. Who knows, maybe these guys making these derogatory remarks about Elvis think their lives are perfect. Sure, we could point out how perfect they are by starting with those two derelicts Elvis had as his stepbrothers. They probably would have done some serious jail time if they had not been

---

■ **TRIVIA ANSWER** / Answer to question on previous page

D.J. Fontana

associated with Elvis. Sure, we could make fun of Lamar Fike, who is obviously a four-hundred-and-fifty-pound glutton, who apparently never exercised any self-control in his entire life. Sure, we could knock Marty Lacker for his catfish looks or the shame he brings on himself every time he opens his mouth. Sure, we could do all of that, but wouldn't that keep them in the Elvis spotlight? I guess they took advantage of the attention some of the fans gave them awhile back and made it a profitable career to bash Elvis and everything he fought so hard to build as an entertainer. Now these guys are celebrities that get rewarded with speaking engage-ments at Elvis events and enjoy huge book sales instead of getting kicked in the ass for tarnishing Elvis's good name and his place in musical his-tory. Incredible!

So thank you, Joe, and your team, for actually doing something about it.

Daniel, I'm sorry for going on a tirade but you asked me what I would tell Joe if I were speaking with him.

That's ok, Jimmy. You're just saying what most people are thinking.

Thanks for giving me a chance to say it.

You're welcome, Jimmy. In closing, what would you like to tell the fans that are out there reading this right now?

That Joe is the best! Check out the website he has. It's unbelievable, and so are the books he has written. I am pretty sure that the *Remember Elvis* book is just as good as the other ones and probably a lot better. Make sure you pick it up.

Thank you for the kind words, Jimmy. Ladies and Gents, a real gentleman, Jimmy Diele from Brooklyn, New York. ♦

■ **TRIVIA QUESTION** / View answer on next page

Which of Elvis's back up vocalists are Grammy award winners?

Always On My Mind

My name is Ricky Cole, and I am currently a Staff Sergeant in the United States Army. I am serving in Balat, Iraq, for ten months. I think how Elvis has influenced me the last few years is through his accomplishments. He is somebody you can really look up to if you're into music. Learning to either sing or learning to play guitar has so much to do with the music that he was involved with. That aura, the style and the things that he did, set a high bar for people to come across. Since I have been over here in Iraq, I've been learning to play guitar, and I've been learning to do a lot of songs from the 50's. It's almost inspirational or spiritual, you know. You start doing something, and then once you realize you can do it, it's like being a kid and learning something new and exciting all over again. When you can do that, it just constantly refreshes you, keeps you open and keeps you going really. It's really fun, and that makes all the difference in the world. Why would you do something that you can't have any fun at? What's the use of really doing it? Elvis will always be an icon for mankind. He will always be my idol. That's for sure. ♦

Did You Know?

Elvis bought Colonel Parker an electric golf cart for one of his birthdays. ♦

■ **TRIVIA ANSWER** / Answer to question on previous page

The Jordanaires

What Really Happened?

Interview Excerpt with Joe Esposito

Reporter: There are rumors when Elvis was in the Army in Germany that Elvis and the Sergeant he was driving for got so cold one night during maneuvers that they pulled a tarp over the Jeep as the engine of the Jeep was running to stay warm. Is it true that the Army used the publicized tonsillitis hospital visit to cover up the fact that Elvis almost died from carbon monoxide poisoning resulting from the fumes that came into the Jeep from a hole in the floorboard?

Joe: Our Unit in Germany used to go into the field quite a bit. One night in the winter, Elvis was out on maneuvers as a scout driver, and he and the Sergeant decided to pull over to the side to take a little nap. So, they covered the jeep with a tarp and left the motor running so they could warm up to the heat of the engine. So, after awhile they passed out from the carbon monoxide gas, which is as you know, quite deadly. Now, here is the strange part. While Elvis and the Sergeant were lying there unconscious, a really strong wind came and blew the tarp off the jeep. That's what saved their lives. That really happened. They didn't pull the tarp off themselves as so many people believe. As for the tonsillitis, well, he got that because of the extreme cold out on maneuvers. So, he went to the hospital to get that taken care of. So, the story that it was a cover up was not true. However, it is true about the gas and the tarp and everything. But the strangest damn thing about it is that the wind blew the tarp off. Talk about divine intervention. ♦

■**TRIVIA QUESTION** / View answer on next page

Who was the only sax player to record with Elvis?

Always On My Mind

Hi, this is Adela Caputo from Salinas, California. Elvis became my dream person from the time I was six years old. I remember seeing him when I was twelve. He was in the movie VIVA LAS VEGAS. From the time I was six until the time I was twelve, on through my teen years into adulthood, he was the only man I found that was so chic, so classy. He was just such a gentleman, just so together that nobody else could touch him. He was just the ultimate of polite and of respect. This was the person any father would want his daughter to bring home. He was the ultimate in a man. I don't think there will ever be another man that comes close to what Elvis was. He will always be in my heart forever. ♦

Did You Know?

Elvis showed up for a birthday party given by Delores Hart for Jan Shepard with a stuffed tiger he called, Danny Boy. ♦

Did You Know?

Elvis was inspired to buy a fleet of motorcycles after Jerry Schilling bought himself a Triumph 650 motorcycle. ♦

■ **TRIVIA ANSWER** / Answer to question on previous page
  Boots Randolph

Ask Joe

I have a letter here from Gaylon Spencer.

Gaylon says:

Dear Joe, there is a picture of Elvis and several of the gang where he is sitting on a gold chair. Behind him, you see Billy Smith, Bill Morris, Lamar Fike, Jerry Schilling, Roy Nixon, Vernon, Charlie Hodge, Sonny, George Klein and Marty Lacker displaying law enforcement badges. Joe, when was this picture taken and why were you not in the picture?

Gaylon, that picture was taken at Christmastime. I cannot remember what year it was. Elvis enjoyed Christmas a lot, and they were all at the house. Elvis was really big into law enforcement badges at the time. To answer your question, I was in California during the holidays spending time with my family and kids. That's why I was not in that picture. It's not like they didn't want me in the shot or anything. I was in California spending Christmas with my children.

Gaylon, don't you think it's amazing that Elvis could get the Sheriff of Memphis and the Mayor of Memphis to come over to the house to hang out during Christmas? That goes to show you the impact Elvis had on anyone that he came in contact with. It did not matter who you were. Gaylon, maybe one day I will add myself to that photo with Photoshop to complete it. What do you think? ♦

■ **TRIVIA QUESTION** / View answer on next page

Who is the only surviving member of the Blue Moon Boys?

Always On My Mind

Hi, my name is Monica Pizano, and I live in Chicago. Elvis Presley has affected me tremendously since the age of nine when my parents first took me to Memphis on a road trip. We visited Graceland. I think that his love for music, his passion and appreciation for it, really comes through. Even at nine years of age, I was just completely impressed with him along with his love for his family. This was what I could really relate to being a child. What probably got me through my teenage years was thinking, "Wow! Elvis did this and Elvis did that. Look at how generous he was. He was always a giving person, giving with his music, giving to charities." He never let people go without. So that's really how he touched my heart and my life. He will always be a part of my life even though I never got to meet him. So now I will introduce you to my daughter, Marina. She is nine and already an Elvis fan. Hold on... "Hello, hi. Elvis Presley, um, I love his music. He was a kind man. He loved kids and I really like his music. He was very generous and always gave to children's hospitals. He is my idol and I love him so much!" ♦

Did You Know?

Elvis received a telegram from the president of Capitol Records inviting him to a cocktail party in Los Angeles on August 24, 1965, to meet the Beatles. ♦

■ **TRIVIA ANSWER** / Answer to question on previous page
Scotty Moore

What Really Happened?

Interview Excerpt with Joe Esposito

Reporter: Diamond Joe, it is widely known that you were sometimes responsible for picking some of the jumpsuits Elvis would be wearing onstage.

Were you included in the discussions that usually took place to go over sketches for jumpsuits Bill Belew wanted to design?

Joe Esposito: Yes, but not just me. It would usually be Charlie, Red and myself among others. Bill Belew would send me all the sketches of jumpsuit ideas he came up with. I would bring the sketches to Elvis. We would all sit down in his office at Graceland or in Los Angeles and go over them. Elvis would pick an outfit and ask, "Well, what do you guys think of this one?" We would tell him what we thought. Some were good and some were bad. Let's face it. So that was basically the process we went through to select a jumpsuit.

How did you set up his jumpsuit wardrobe for the tours?

Well, for the tours, we would always bring a lot of jumpsuits with us, ok?

For instance, if we were scheduled to do a ten-day tour, we would at a minimum always bring 30 of them. Elvis would have enough variety to fit his taste or mood for any particular engagement. The jumpsuits would always travel in these big custom-made cases that were big enough to hang them in. Once we got to the hotel, we would then have a room that we would keep these cases in.

■ **TRIVIA QUESTION** / View answer on next page

Which person closest to Elvis christened his plastic 26-foot rowboat "Gladys" in honor of Elvis's mother?

Elvis would usually go into this room and pick the outfit he wanted to wear. I need to mention that Elvis always picked his own jumpsuits for a show. That is something we never did. He usually did this the day before a show. We would have it ready and laid out for him in his bedroom when he got up in the afternoon of the show. ♦

Up Close and Personal: Upstairs at Graceland

A candid conversation between Joe Esposito and Daniel Lombardy

Daniel: Let's talk about the Elvis bedroom. What was the main color used in the bedroom?

Joe: Elvis liked red a lot, red or blue. You could also see the red and black combination. Since he usually slept during the day, he preferred to have his room nice and dark where he slept. So you could usually see the combinations red and black, or blue and white. Like everyone else, he would go through different color phases and combinations throughout his life. I can remember that most often you could see his room decorated in red and black during the winter, and blue and white during the summertime. ♦

Did You Know?

Joe Guercio was the musical director of the International when he first worked with Elvis. ♦

■ **TRIVIA ANSWER** / Answer to question on previous page

Colonel Parker

What Really Happened?

Interview Excerpt with Joe Esposito

Reporter: Was Elvis concerned by how the public might perceive the '68 COMEBACK SPECIAL since his entire future was riding on a successful outcome of this particular show?

Joe Esposito: Well, like I have said before, he was definitely concerned when he started making the special because he never did a TV special before. It was a first time thing for him. He only had one shot to do it right. You have to remember that he was not in front of the public for seven or eight years before that special came out. So he didn't know how it was going to be accepted by the public. So you can imagine how thrilled Elvis was when he got the highest ratings on TV for that year, especially after receiving lackluster turnouts for his later movies at the box office. The '68 Special made him feel really special. People still loved him and wanted to see him. You have to remember that something like that is very important to an entertainer. That is probably one of your biggest concerns most of the time. "Do they still love me? Am I still hot?" You know? So by pulling off such a successful special, Elvis definitely squashed any doubts there might have been out there about him and his future as the King of Rock 'n' Roll. That's for sure. ♦

Did You Know?

Vernon, at one point, worked as a cement finisher. ♦

■ **TRIVIA QUESTION** / View answer on next page

In which Elvis movie does a young lady play the drums, and what was her name?

What Really Happened?

Interview Excerpt with Joe Esposito

Reporter: While Elvis was in California in the 70's, he witnessed two guys fighting at a gas station. It's said that Elvis stopped the car, got out and broke up the fight. What do you recall about this event?

Joe Esposito: The guys told me that they were with him. It's a true story. He told the guys, "Stop! Pull into the gas station." He jumped out of the car. He was very nice about it. He went over and said, "Guys, you know, stop it!" Naturally, that stopped it immediately when they saw that it was Elvis Presley saying this to them. That's what really stopped the fight. Elvis said, "You know, this is not right. It's not good for you guys." They just could not believe that Elvis Presley had stopped this fight. It did end right there. They all went their separate ways. Elvis got back in the car and drove off. ♦

Always On My Mind

My name is Tally Lauriti. I'm in Highland, California. Elvis has been a part of my life, geez, since I've been six years old, since the first time I ever saw him on KING CREOLE. I always try to wear my hair like his, always tried to live my life in a big way, the way I thought he'd live his life, you know, mom and apple pie. I'm always trying to be generous and good to people the way he was. Elvis was a wonderful and kind person. I mean, I can't picture my life without him. My whole life had something to do with Elvis at one time or another. I always thought about him like a member of the family. ♦

■ **TRIVIA ANSWER** / Answer to question on previous page
SPINOUT, Deborah Walley

Ask Joe

I have a letter here from David Morgan in Japan.

David says:

I read one time that Elvis had met Bruce Lee several times. I was wondering why there were no pictures of this? I believe that a picture with both of them together would have been awesome. Also, I wondered if Elvis ever met Marilyn Monroe? If so, why doesn't a picture of them exist?

All right, David. Elvis did meet Bruce Lee a few times, but in those days, people weren't walking around with cameras the way they do today. We bumped into him on the studio a lot while both of them were making movies. Elvis was very honored to meet Bruce Lee because he was such a great martial arts expert. As you know, Elvis was really into Karate. So to meet someone as remarkable as Bruce Lee was very special for him. Regarding Elvis meeting Marilyn, yes, they did meet. Once before Elvis went into the Army and then again at Paramount Studios in 1960. They talked for a few minutes, but they never had an affair. David, the same reason of why there are no photos would also apply here; namely that people didn't walk around with cameras the way they do today. ♦

Did You Know?

Colonel Parker served with the 64th Regiment of the Coast Guard Artillery in Fort Shafter, Honolulu. ♦

■ **TRIVIA QUESTION** / View answer on next page

Who introduced Elvis to Anita Wood and traveled with him to West Germany?

What Really Happened?

Interview Excerpt with Joe Esposito

Reporter: Joe, what do you recall when Elvis was recording the song "Surrender"? What inspired Elvis to want to record that particular song, and how did that come about?

Joe Esposito: That song came about one day when Freddy Bienstock who ran Elvis's publishing company came to the studio with a few demos and played them for Elvis. Once Elvis heard that particular song, he immediately took a liking to it and said, "Hell yeah! I'm recording it." And he did. Watching this particular session was a lot of fun because you have to understand that Elvis's studio sessions were like personal concerts. To hear him sing this song during a session was just out of this world. It was always so much fun just to watch this gentleman sing behind his microphone, just having a ball with all of the musicians and singers around him. He really felt strong about ballads and melodic pieces. He would sing up a storm and have a good time, as was the case with the making and recording of *Surrender*. ♦

Did You Know?

Colonel Parker arranged for a special Mother's Day radio show broadcast at stations across the country, playing songs such as: *Crying In The Chapel* and *His Hand In Mine* among others. ♦

■ **TRIVIA ANSWER** / Answer to question on previous page

Cliff Gleaves

Fan Spotlight Interview

With Ashley Brooks

My name is Ashley Brooks, and I'm from Cedartown, Georgia. I'm twenty-three. Oh Lord, I'm twenty-four. That's right [laughs]. I'm twenty-four. I just had a birthday.

Daniel Lombardy: [laughing] That's ok. Happy Birthday, Ashley.

Thank you. I started really getting into Elvis probably just a year ago, maybe a little bit longer. I did not have the same kind of exposure to Elvis as some people had. Since then, I've gotten lots of books and movies. I'm really into the documentaries. The one I love is THAT'S THE WAY IT IS. I watch it about once a week.

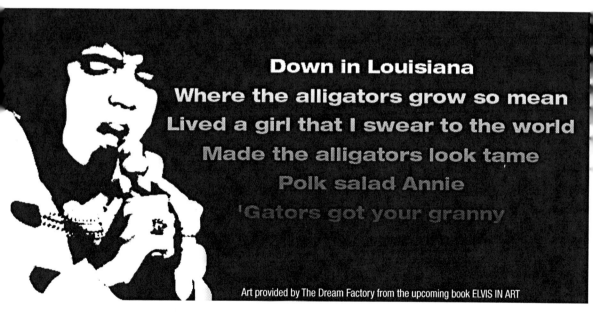

**Down in Louisiana
Where the alligators grow so mean
Lived a girl that I swear to the world
Made the alligators look tame
Polk salad Annie
'Gators got your granny**

Art provided by The Dream Factory from the upcoming book ELVIS IN ART

■ **TRIVIA QUESTION** / View answer on next page

What was the name of the hospital Lisa Marie was born in; and which Memphis hospital was originally considered?

I absolutely love the ballads that he did in the later years. Those really get to me. You can just hear the soul and the love in his voice when he's singing those. That's pretty much all I ever listen to. I go from one CD to the next everyday. I just never get tired of his music. It's part of my soul and my life. Everybody at work calls me little Elvis. They try to pay me to do an impression, but of course, that's not going to happen.

Why not?

Well, it's because the last time I did an Elvis impression, I couldn't walk for two days.

[Laughing]

I pulled a leg muscle [laughing]

That's too funny Ashley. Tell me what would you tell Joe if he was on the phone with you right now?

I'm sorry?

What would you tell Joe if you were on the phone with him right now?

Mostly, really, that I really appreciate the website and all he's done to introduce Elvis to all of us that weren't there for all of the things that were going on while Elvis was still with us. If it wasn't for the website and all of Joe's hard work, I don't think I would know near as much as I do now or even be as big a fan as I am. He opens the doors and let's you into a personal side of Elvis that only a few have seen.

■ **TRIVIA ANSWER** / Answer to question on previous page

Baptist Hospital, Methodist Hospital

Well said, Ashley. Is there anything you would like to share with the other Elvis fans that are reading this?

Just that I hope that Elvis had as much an impact on their lives as he has on mine. Even in this short period that I've been an Elvis fan, Elvis music is my stress reliever. It's my happy music and my sad music when I'm lonely or when I'm upset. I will often put in a CD. No matter what is happening, or if something went wrong, it will always bring a smile to my face. I hope that Elvis does the same thing for everybody else listening to his music.

That was very nicely put, Ashley. You're a good person and a great fan. Ladies and Gentleman, Ashley Brooks from Cedartown, Georgia. ♦

Always On My Mind

My name is Gina Wilson, and I'm from Longview, Washington. I just want to say, Elvis, you have been part of my life ever since I can remember. I remember being five years old sitting in front of the television during the ALOHA FROM HAWAII special and being mesmerized at the TV. My mom said it was time for me to go to bed, and I wouldn't leave the TV. I wanted to wait until the show was over. Your music has been very inspirational to me. It's very soothing. It comforts me when I've had a bad day. It keeps me happy when I'm having a good day. I feel like you have always been a friend that I can always count on. I just turn that TV on, and you're there for me. I miss you terribly! I really wish you were still here. ♦

■ **TRIVIA QUESTION** / View answer on next page

Who coined the following phrase, "If you are not an Elvis fan, no explanation is possible. If you are an Elvis fan, no explanation is necessary?"

Up Close and Personal:
Elvis the Avid Reader

A candid conversation between Joe Esposito and Daniel Lombardy

Daniel: Tell me about Elvis being an avid reader. I know that people have the impression that Elvis was not well-educated or well-read. What are your thoughts about that?

Joe: Elvis got into reading a lot because he always had this thing in his mind as to why he was picked to be this fantastically talented entertainer with the charisma that drew all the people to him. So he started reading a lot of different books about very gifted and mysterious people to help enlighten him about why he was put here on this earth. So he started getting into books that covered the paranormal and the unexplained. He was very much into that. He always thought there had to be more than just us in the universe. So he started pondering if people from other planets came to visit us once and awhile. Elvis also believed in reincarnation. Even though he was a very religious person, he truly believed that he was on this earth before but he could not remember when. I can remember, one time, there was an article in the paper about this statue they found in some country someplace. I looked at the profile of the statue. I'm telling you, it was Elvis. It was amazing! Elvis kept saying, "See, I told you I was here before. Look! Look!"

I know it sounds strange, but that is a true story. That really happened. Like I said, he read books that would give him answers as to why he was here. He wouldn't just read them once, he would read them over

■ **TRIVIA ANSWER** / Answer to question on previous page
Originally coined by Dr. Lester Hoffman, made popular by George Klein

and over again, make little notes right in the margins, and try to take the meaning of things apart. So he would go back over them again and again to make sure he got everything he could out of those books. As anyone can tell you that ever got a book from Elvis, you would see all the little notes inside of it, little comments and stuff. Even though Elvis read, he would never read novels. The books that got his interest had to do with the meaning of life and that sort of thing. He was always trying to figure out how things worked in life. I'll tell you something else. We used to carry a portable bookcase with us while we were on tour.

Really?

Yes, it was a portable bookcase, covered in leather and everything. We used to go on tour with it.

That's amazing. When did he find the time to read while you guys were living it up and carrying on around him?

He would do most of his reading in his bedroom. Once he closed that door, nobody bothered him. He'd go in there and read at different times. He didn't do any of this in the 60's. We were just too busy making all those movies; sometimes three a year along with other things we had going on. He started getting into reading toward the end of the 60's, with all of the traveling we did all over the place, crashing at 5 o'clock in the morning and reading for a few hours. He would often read on the bed that you see on the Lisa Marie.

■ **TRIVIA QUESTION** / View answer on next page

Where did D.J. Fontana meet Elvis?

With all of the reading Elvis was doing, did you ever see him wearing reading glasses?

No, he had really great eyesight.

Did Elvis ever read to you from the books he was into?

Oh sure. He did that all the time. He would usually come across something in a book and do a big elaborate presentation about it with all the effects and everything. Some of those readings were really interesting. ♦

Always On My Mind

Hi, my name is Jacqueline Raphael. I live in Basel, Switzerland. I am very, very happy and proud to be an Elvis fan. I've been an Elvis fan since I was ten years old. I saw Elvis on the ALOHA FROM HAWAII special. Since then, I have been an Elvis fan. I even opened up an Elvis fan club here in Switzerland called the Elvis Show Fan Club. This fan club brought me all over the world. I've seen Joe in different places, like in Vegas, Germany and in Vienna. I saw him all over the world. "Joe, we are so happy and proud to know you, and we hope that we can stay in touch. We thank you for everything that you have done for Elvis and what you are still doing. You were the right guy for Elvis. I hope to see you soon again here. I would like to invite you again to Switzerland to have you be with our Elvis fans. Take care of yourself. Take care of your health and everything. We want you for a long, long time. We want to see you around in the world everywhere! We Love You!" ♦

■ **TRIVIA ANSWER** / Answer to question on previous page
Louisiana Hayride

What Really Happened?

Interview Excerpt with Joe Esposito

Reporter: It is rumored that during the time of the Circle G Ranch, Elvis went on a truck buying spree that included buying trucks for everyone that was present. Is it true that Elvis actually gave a truck away to the truck salesman and then tried to give him another one shortly thereafter?

Joe Esposito: Well, that is true. Elvis, when he did things, he would go crazy with it. We were all ranchers now all of a sudden. So we all had to have pickup trucks because that's what ranchers had in those days. Just imagine us trying to be rugged and having straw sticking out of our mouths and all that. So anyway, he started buying trucks for everybody because he was just so giving. He bought one for the electrician that was doing some electrical work for us and the carpenter. He got one for the painter, and he even tried to give one to the salesman that we bought the trucks from!

Of course the salesman had to turn it down with, "I appreciate you wanting to give me this fine truck but I can't accept it, Elvis." So Elvis did in fact try giving him a truck. He didn't try it twice like some people said. He only tried it once. Quite frankly, I don't think that Elvis recognized the gentleman as being the salesman who sold us the trucks previously. ◆

■ **TRIVIA QUESTION** / View answer on next page

Which former dancer directed two of Elvis's movies, and what were the two titles?

Ask Joe

I have a letter here from A.J.

A.J. says:

I read that Billy Smith and Marty Lacker said Elvis made another handwritten will leaving many of the Memphis Mafia some things. Billy said you put it in your briefcase, but Vernon didn't know about that will and never used it because you hid it. Joe, can you tell me the truth about this story.

A.J., well you know there are a lot of rumors out there about a lot of different things. It's really hard for me to believe that Billy Smith would say something like that since he was there and actually knows what really happened. Marty, on the other hand, was not around during this so he would have no idea of what went on in the first place. So don't worry about what he says. Let's say this obvious work of fiction actually existed. Why would I hide it if members of the Memphis Mafia were being left something? That doesn't make any sense at all. What would be the point? Why would I do that?

To wrap up and put this rumor to rest, I will tell you flat out that this handwritten will never existed except in someone's imagination. I would stake my life on it. As for the real will made out by Elvis, it was in fact witnessed by Billy Smith and I believe Elvis's girlfriend at the time, Ginger Alden. Sorry, there was no other will. ♦

What Really Happened?

Interview Excerpt with Joe Esposito

Reporter: Joe, tell us about your family when you were growing up in Chicago before you went into the Army?

Joe Esposito: Well, I came from a very good Italian family, not wealthy just middle class. My dad, Frank Esposito, was just a mechanic for the Chicago Transit Authority. I have an older sister, Phyllis. My mom, Antoinette, worked in a factory making Zenith radios at that time. My sister is about three and a half years older than me. I also have a brother, Frank. He's about a year and a half older than me. We just had a good family. We were living in an all-Italian neighborhood, a lot of socializing, having a great time in life, enjoying life. It was just nice. I hung out with a great bunch of guys back home. Those days back in the 50's, you remember, were nice days. There were no problems, no drugs around. It was just a lot of fun, music, beer drinking and having a good time in the neighborhood. The schools were fabulous. Those were such great years the 50's. I'm so happy that I was raised during that era; especially if you think about the major turns the world has taken since then. I was very fortunate to have experienced that era. ♦

Did You Know?

The former name for Circle G Ranch was Twinkletown Farm. ♦

■ **TRIVIA QUESTION** / View answer on next page

In which movie did a former Ms. America play opposite Elvis?

Fan Spotlight Interview

With Andrea Stoeckle

My name is Andie Stoeckle. I'm from San Mateo, California. What got me into Elvis and everything is Elvis, of course. Back in the 50's, when he first came out, I was just a little tike. One of the major reasons he infatuated me was because of my aunt. She was a huge fan of his. I mean she was totally in love with him. She made sure I got plenty of Presley exposure frequently. So it was just a matter of time before I, like many, started dreaming about growing up and marrying Elvis Presley. You know? I can still remember seeing him at the Cow Palace on November 10, 1970. That's when I really started panting over him like every woman in the place. He was just such a wonderful, wonderful person and so beautiful to look at. Like I said before, I think, read and listen to him every single day. So no day goes by without Elvis being in my life in some way. I mean he has really done a pretty good number on me let me tell you. Just ask my husband. I just wish Elvis were still around so I could just thank him. I would just love to thank him and just put my arms around him. He was just such a wonderful person.

Daniel Lombardy: Andie, what would you consider your favorite Elvis movies and songs. What do you enjoy listening to?

Daniel, I've been playing his *Elvis is Back* CD recently. I have to say that one of my favorite songs on that CD is *What A Night*. When you hear Elvis singing that song, you can actually see him singing that song. He's just so sexy when he sings that one. My number one favorite Elvis

---

It was a night
oo-oo what a night
It was it really was such a night
The moon was bright
oh how so bright
It was it really was such a night

Art provided by The Dream Factory from the upcoming book ELVIS IN ART

movie is JAILHOUSE ROCK. I also love the movie because Elvis has a line in it that is a knockout. Can you guess which line?

"The beast in me" line.

That's right! You got it. "You know, it's not tactics. It's the beast in me."

[Laughs]

Yeah, I just love that. It's so raw. It's so Elvis. I mean, I just play that over and over and over. That movie I think is the greatest. I just love it so much. I would say that the *Wonder of You* is a close second, but there's just something about the song *Such a Night* and the phrase, "The beast in me," that I love.

■ **TRIVIA QUESTION** / View answer on next page
Which one of Elvis's band members made it into the Guinness Book of World Records and what was the reason?

What about your favorite Elvis movies?

My favorite movie, like I said, is JAILHOUSE ROCK.

Ah, yeah, that's right. JAILHOUSE ROCK went right over my head! [laughing]

And my name is Daniel Lombardy… [laughing]… just kidding.

It's all right. [laughs] Just a little slow today. That's all.

Aren't we all? [Laughing] Oh my God! This is too funny! [laughing]

We should tone this down a bit so nobody gets the idea that this is a conversation between two cross-eyed boneheads or something.

Yeah, can't have people thinking we got dain bramage. How would that make us look right?

What??? Oh yeah, the brain damage thing. That's right, Andie! Can't have them thinking we got peanut brittle between our ears.

That's right.

Glad we got all that cleared up, right?

Yep.

Andie, if Joe were on the telephone with us right now, what would you tell him?

■ **TRIVIA ANSWER** / Answer to question on previous page

J.D. Sumner for having the deepest bass voice.

What would I tell him? Oh, you know what! I was thinking about Joe Esposito the other day. If he were on the phone right now, I would just like to thank him over and over and over again for what a wonderful job he's doing on the TCB Joe website, and answering all those terrible rumors with Fact or Fiction. I would just love to thank him. That's it really. He's just such a wonderful man. Keep up the good work because we need to hear all the positive things. Who else but Joe knows every-thing about Elvis. So thank you, Joe! Thank you for everything. We really appreciate you as the great person who has allowed us to get to know you by connecting with us personally and through your ongoing efforts to educate the fans about who Elvis really was.

What are some of the thoughts you would like to share with the other fans reading this?

Oh, the fans, let's see. If they could hear my thoughts, I just wish some of the younger fans could really get to know the real Elvis and not the monster Marty, Lamar, Billy, and some of the others made him out to be. It's really sad that they would want to degrade a person when he is no longer here to defend himself and smudging his image.

I also want the fans to know that there is so much more to Elvis Pre-sley than him just being this amazing rocker. There is still so much to discover, so much to learn. Elvis has left behind a body of work that is absolutely mind-boggling. When I sometimes look at pictures of Elvis, I see the rings on his finger, all of his chains, his medallions, his hats and his clothing. Then I compare his dress to the kids and musicians

---

■ **TRIVIA QUESTION** / View answer on next page

Which one of Elvis's co-stars would eventually have her own TV show?

of today. You know what? They are expressing themselves in the same dramatic way that Elvis was doing way back in the 50's and 60's. The most important thing I would like to tell the Elvis fans is to keep your mind open and continue keeping Elvis in your heart and in your mind regardless of the negative crap you hear and read from people whose character has already been determined to be hateful and hopeless. Support Joe and the few remaining people like him that are keeping up their efforts to keep Elvis's good image and reputation in tact for the next generation. ♦

Always On My Mind

This is Rhonda McKinney from Lynchburg, Tennessee. I've listened to Elvis all of my life. I've listened to his music and watched his movies. Just to see him on the TV and in the movies, your heart just stops. You think, my goodness, what a wonderful person he really truly was. Then, when you listen to the words to the songs, they just make you feel so good. You can forget about what's going on around you, especially when you're having a bad day. Listening to him will make you feel better. Then you can watch a movie, and it can make you laugh or it could make you cry. That'll make you feel better too. I wish I could have gotten the chance to see him in person. I never did but at least I have the memory of his music. That is something I will always treasure, always. ♦

What Really Happened?

Interview Excerpt with Joe Esposito

Reporter: Do you ever remember any fans going to great lengths to get to the floor Elvis was on at the hotels and stuff like that?

Joe Esposito: Yes. We were doing IT HAPPENED AT THE WORLD'S FAIR in Seattle, Washington. I forget the name of the hotel we were staying in. It was a tall, old, classy hotel. So we'd be upstairs just sitting around watching television late in the evening. We didn't go out in the evenings too much because we worked all day shooting the movie. We'd sit down, have dinner upstairs in the suite and watch a little TV. All of a sudden, one of the guys said, "I hear some noise." He looked out the window and then opened the window. There were two girls out there looking in the window! Now, we were 12 stories up, ok!

Was there a balcony?

No, they climbed up the fire escape outside the window! This was right by the living room window of the suite we were in. That scared the hell out of us because we didn't realize how the hell they got up there. After awhile, we realized that they climbed up the fire escape. Elvis was very nice about it. He opened up the window and let them in. Elvis was telling them, "You know that was very dangerous girls. Something could have happened or somebody could have gotten upset

---

■ **TRIVIA QUESTION** / View answer on next page

Which one of Elvis's co-stars in the '68 COMEBACK SPECIAL also played a small role as a mermaid in one of his movies?

and called the police as soon as you walked by their window." Luckily, everything was fine. So they were just thrilled to death that they did that and got to see their idol. Elvis was very nice to them, talked for a while and signed a couple of autographs. Then, they went out the door. That was it. The cops outside the door couldn't believe their eyes when these girls walked by them because they never saw any girls walk into the suite. All of a sudden, two girls come strolling out of the suite! Can you imagine the sheer panic that must have struck deep into their hearts, considering they were in charge of Elvis's security and everything? So it was very interesting when that happened. ♦

Did You Know?

Vernon bought a four bedroom house from Orville Bean, the same man that sent him and Gladys's brother to prison for uttering a forged instrument. They apparently altered a four-dollar check from Orville in payment for a hog. ♦

Up Close and Personal: Recording in the Studio

A candid conversation between Joe Esposito and Daniel Lombardy

Daniel: Do you ever remember Elvis feeling pressure to perform in the recording studio? Did he ever get nervous knowing what was at stake?

Joe: Recording sessions were great. He was never nervous at a recording session because he was not in front of an audience. He was just in front of his band members, the singers, the engineers and his producer, Felton Jarvis.

Let me tell you. They were really great sessions. I tell people all the time that I was one of the very few people ever to witness the number of Elvis concerts that I did.

You have to remember, Elvis's recording sessions were dress rehearsals for his concerts. So you would be seeing him and his singers go through the motions of generating the ideas to put into the shows. You would see him suggest that the singers do this, or have him direct Ronnie Tutt into doing that with the drums. You see, back then, all of the performers were in the same room, not like today. It was really great to see all of that. When you were there, you would see them go over something over and over until it was right for the show. It was so much fun to watch this happening, a lot of great memories. Now to hear Elvis sing a song that you knew was going to be a hit, while it was being recorded, is of course an unforgettable event. I am very honored to have been around him while all of that was happening. When I hear a certain Elvis song today, I don't remember him singing it on stage. I remember him singing it during the recording session. So it's a completely different situation with me. His recording sessions were the best. ♦

■ **TRIVIA QUESTION** / View answer on next page
Which former Elvis girlfriend has a son that is now a famous Hollywood actor?

What Really Happened?

Interview Excerpt with Joe Esposito

Reporter: It has been said that Elvis would often get into character no matter what he was into at the time. During the Circle G Ranch, he was a rancher. Can you remember any other times that Elvis would dress for the part so to speak?

Joe Esposito: Well, you know, he was always like that. He always wanted to dress for what he was doing at the time. That is true. That is why I say, when we played football, we would go out and buy football jerseys and all that kind of stuff. If it was roller-skating, he had to go out and buy everybody roller skates. I am trying to remember the time we started to wear leather jackets. He played a pilot in the movie IT HAPPENED AT THE WORLD'S FAIR. That's what he did. If he was into something like the Circle G, he would go crazy and really get into it all the way. He went out and bought chaps, nice western jackets and cowboy boots for everybody. He just went as far as he could go. He got us all trailers. He was like that with everything he did in his life. Same thing happened with the jumpsuits. He immediately had dozens designed in all kinds of different designs and themes. That was another example of how he was when he went all the way. Yeah, we were all cowboys for a long time there at Circle G. We were real shitkickers.

Are you being serious, Joe?

Of course! You turned into a real rancher at Circle G. You enjoyed fresh cow manure in the air and donkey shit on your shoe. ♦

■ **TRIVIA ANSWER** / Answer to question on previous page
Sheila Ryan Caan. Her son, Scott Caan, starred in movies like BOILER ROOM, OCEANS ELEVEN, OCEANS TWELVE, and GONE IN SIXTY SECONDS to name only a few.

[46]

Always On My Mind

My name is Jeffro Blues. I am originally from Lower Alabama. Elvis has always been the main inspiration in my life along with the old blues and soul singers and the early country guys. Elvis was the main thing. I just miss him so much. I just love him. I want everybody out there that hasn't heard Elvis to at least listen and give him a chance. I know that once you hear him, you're going to see why he is what he is, what he was and what he will always be. ♦

Ask Joe

I have a letter here from Andie Stoeckle.

Andie says:

Hi Joe, I've always wanted to know if Elvis ever asked Linda Thompson to get married? She was one of the longest live-in girlfriends. At least, that is what I have read. I often wondered why those two never got married.

Well, yes, Elvis and Linda were very close, very much so. I don't think he ever asked her to get married because we would have heard about it. Linda never said he did, but they were very close. She was a wonderful lady for Elvis. You know, they spent a lot of time together. I think, after awhile, Linda knew it wasn't going to go anywhere. She better go out and get her own life going. That's what she did. They stayed friends after they broke up. She is a wonderful lady. I still stay in touch with her all the time now. She loved Elvis tremendously, and he loved her too. ♦

■ **TRIVIA QUESTION** / View answer on next page

What was the name of the lady that welcomed Elvis back to the states from Germany on behalf of her famous father?

Fan Spotlight Interview

With Juanita Pasquini

My name is Juanita Pasquini, and I'm from Albany, New York.

I loved Elvis ever since I was a little girl. My exposure to Elvis came through my parents, who really loved him. My mom, when she was a young gal, never took to anybody but she loved Elvis. She still remembers wearing the pin that said, "I love Elvis" on her coat and listening to the albums. Then, when Elvis died, I was just so saddened. I remember being twelve years old. I can remember the day. I remember my parents and my family's reaction. From that point on, I really got more into Elvis. My husband, when I got married, well, I've been with my husband for ten years and we've been married seven, was not into Elvis. Well, guess what?

What? [Laughs]

Well, I have him schooled and groomed as a genuine Elvis fan. Now he is going around saying, "Oh, my God! You're speaking with this guy Daniel that is Joe's right hand, the very Joe Esposito you are always talking about." This is Charlie Hodge, you know, this is this one, and this is that one. So he knows all the important people that were around Elvis and I'm saying, "Oh, my God! This is so scary!"

His favorite song is *If I Can Dream,* and he's just knocked out by the '68 COMEBACK SPECIAL.

■ **TRIVIA ANSWER** / Answer to question on previous page
Nancy Sinatra

**There must be lights
burning brighter somewhere
Got to be birds flying higher
in a sky more blue
If I can dream of a better land
Where all my brothers
walk hand in hand**

Art provided by The Dream Factory from the upcoming book ELVIS IN ART

He's just in awe of it. I remember the first time he watched that special. He was like, "Oh my Lord! People out there don't realize how awesome this man was." Daniel, I think it's really cool he took to Elvis the way he did. So every year when we go on vacation, we stockpile a bunch of stuff, just stuff that we are going to do like videos and a bunch of books. So this past year, we took Joe's, HIS BEST FRIEND REMEMBERS video, the one he had done on Elvis. We have the '68 COMEBACK SPECIAL DVD. We watched both the full-length ALOHA FROM HAWAII show and the ALTERNATE ALOHA CONCERT, the basic practice concert they did. So every year, we have like a couple of days that we call our Elvisfests. Daniel, I'm sure you have figured out that my husband and I are just hooked on Elvis, and we are real die-hards, die-hard Elvis fans.

■ **TRIVIA QUESTION** / View answer on next page

Who was the person that mentioned Elvis to Sam Phillips?

Nothing wrong with that, Juanita, but isn't your being such a huge fan the point of us talking in the first place?

Yes, you're absolutely right! I just wanted to make sure you knew you were not talking with a nut ball or anything.

No worries. I don't hear the telltale "I'm TinkerBell, and I served Elvis coffee just this last week in Wyoming" signs coming from you [Laughing].

You're a riot, Danny.

You want me to be quiet?

No, I said you're a riot.

Oh [Laughing]

[Laughing] You know my husband and I were at a wedding recently that had an Elvis song playing. Everyone was saying that it was Elvis singing and that he sounded great. We got into a debate. I said, "No, that's not Elvis." Then, my husband gets sucked into it and said, "If my wife says it's not Elvis Presley, it's not Elvis Presley! This woman is a genuine Elvis lover! She has posters all over the house. Hell, I can't even use the bathroom without having Elvis looking back at me from the shower curtain! She absolutely loves that man! So the person singing that song is NOT Elvis." That shut up everybody. See what my man does for me?

Yep, he put on a cape, swooped in and did the tornado dance on 'em.

Daniel, I know this is going to sound so crazy, but I lost my dad and my stepdad over the past five, six years. I was telling my husband that usually when you die, a person that was important comes and takes you away. I wonder who's going to take me away? My husband looks at me and he goes, "Are you kidding me?" He says, "Elvis Presley is going to come and friggin' take you!"

[Laughing]

I laughed so hard because I thought that was so sweet. He says, "Elvis is going to be there." He'll say, "Honey, you're late! Where ya been?"

[Laughing]

That has meant so much to me. He said to me, honest to God, "I have never seen anybody who has such a deep love and appreciation for an artist and their work like you have with Elvis." He said, "I never ever saw that in anybody else who was a fan of another group or other artist." When we go to our summer camp, which is about seven hours away, we both bring our entire stash of our favorite CDs. Of course, I bring a ton of my Elvis CDs that I keep on my side of the car, and he has his. On the way to our cabin, we listen to nothing but Elvis. Then, on the way back, I let him play all of the stuff that he likes. So he can expose me to more things that he likes, since he's into everything. I'm just so thrilled that I was lucky enough to marry a man that now loves Elvis as much as I do.

■ **TRIVIA QUESTION** / View answer on next page

Who was the songwriter that wrote more songs for Elvis than anyone?

Sounds like you are very fortunate, Juanita.

Yes, I am, Danny. I've been entering the contest. I was telling him about it, how it's with Joe, you go to Vegas and Graceland and it's for two people. He said, "I actually have to tell you that I was never one for contests or anything like that, but, oh my God! That was one I had to enter." My husband told me, "If you win that contest, I could bring you back home and bury you because that would be it for the rest of your life. You wouldn't want anything else in your life but that!" I told him, "Yes, you're right. I would be ready to die then."

[Laughing]

That would really be it. Yes, I love Elvis. He's my boy. He's always been my boy. People crack up. They say, "You like Elvis?" I say, "Don't you say anything about my boy, or you'll get slapped so hard, your eyes will water up!"

[Laughing]

Oh yeah. I would make sure their cheeks would stay glowing and numb for a good ten or twenty minutes. Nobody talks bad about my boy.

Damn! I can just see someone holding their cheek with tears in their eyes looking at you in disbelief.

I'm known for my love of Elvis at work. The people I work with always say that it's amazing that I like Elvis so much. I tell them, "Have a seat. You need some schooling! Now, we'll start you off with *Burning Love*. It's a wonderful piece that will…"

■ **TRIVIA ANSWER** / Answer to question on previous page

Ben Weisman

[Laughs]

Don't laugh. That's true. They have to listen to it two hundred thirty-one times in a row to get the full flavor of the whole thing. Just joking of course. I do have to tell you something weird. Can I tell you this without you laughing at me?

Hold on a second. Let me get down from my handstand. Ok, I'm ready.

Well, I currently have a patient with her leg all busted up that used to be in the military back in the 70's. She has her leg all busted up and what not. We're talking about different performers who you'd like to see. She brought her daughter to see Cher. She was saying that she was very surprised at how amazing the show was that Cher put on and everything. Yet, she said, "By far, the most amazing show I have ever seen was in the military." Back in the military, her boss told her, "I want you to be the driver and escort for this big Colonel who is going to be attending a big benefit that is going to be held someplace over the weekend." She said, "No, I don't want to do it. I don't want to do it." And he says, "I promise you will get perks down the road for it." So she eventually says, "Fine." So she's driving the Colonel. They go to this big benefit concert that has different artists there over the weekend. There was supposed to be a top-notch surprise guest. She's indifferent. The Colonel said, "No, I would like you to come in and watch the show too since you were kind enough to drive me." So she is sitting next to him, when they finally announce that the time had come to present the surprise artist.

■ **TRIVIA QUESTION** / View answer on next page

Which Mark James song would play a significant part in Elvis's stage show?

She is sitting there watching the stage, expecting Lawrence Welk or Big Bird to come out. She keeps watching the stage and out walks this guy that looked like Elvis Presley! Could it be?

She says, "I about fell over from the heat flash that came over me!" She said, "He was just incredible, almost impossible to describe. Even before he opened his mouth, you go Oh my God! Oh my god! [Screams] E L V I S!!!!!! Hey baby, I'm here in the front row."

She said, "Oh my God! He had this aura, this charisma that just oozed from him." She's saying, "Yeah man. That's Elvis! That's friggin' Elvis Presley!" She says, "The place just came undone. The people went nuts! Absolute pandemonium! You couldn't even imagine the frenzy and noise that literally shook that place."

UNBELIEVABLE

So I am sitting there, figuring out how to bust up her other leg because I'm getting more and more jealous by the minute. She goes on, gets back to work on Monday and has a conversation with her boss; you know the one that pawned this supposed unimportant errand on her. The boss is saying, "You know, I'm really glad you came through on that thing over the weekend. That really helped out a lot. You're a team player, great sport." She told him, "Are you kidding me? I will never forget this weekend as long as I live!" He asks, "Why? What happened?" She responds, "Do you have any idea of who the surprise guest was?"

■ **TRIVIA ANSWER** / Answer to question on previous page

Suspicious Minds

He has no idea. She says, "It was Elvis Presley!" All of the color drained out of his face and his jaw dropped! She almost had to hold this grown man up! It was like she was witnessing what a person goes through the moment they make the biggest mistake of their lives. Well, it was one of those moments. He said, "You are not going to do that to me. Tell me you're kidding. I am about to throw myself off the roof this morning!"

She goes on drilling this boss into the ground with it. He was so cool, better than in the magazines. He is mumbling, "I should have driven him myself. I should have been more inquisitive. I had it and gave it away." He asks, "You really saw Elvis?" She says, "Honey, I was in the front row. You think listening to him on the radio and the albums is good?" She said, "You just don't know what this guy has." She said, "He's got something that no one else has."

She said, "My boss was kicking himself for a good year after that."

Daniel, she tells her grandkids that she got to see the man. She is in her sixties now. She says, "I got to see the man who started all this. No one else in the business does what he does. I got to see him." I'm hearing this and I want to kill myself. I'm so jealous!

You crack me up. [Laughing]

So she says, "Juanita, that was the highlight of my Army career, seeing Elvis on that weekend, where I begged my boss not to brush that task off on me and make me do it. My boss was physically kicking himself,

---

■ **TRIVIA QUESTION** / View answer on next page

Which former member of the Starlite Wranglers would later go on to play a significant role in Elvis's life?

crumpling and destroying stuff in the office. He really looked bad after a week of this." He said later, "If I could turn back the clock, I would have carried the Colonel to the concert on my back, if I would have known Elvis was going to be there!" I was telling that story to my husband and he said, "Damn!"

Daniel, Elvis is my boy.

That's right. He's your boy.

It's that simple.

There you have it. Great story. Sorry for laughing like I was on crazy pills. That guy must have felt like he had the winning Powerball ticket for $500 Million, gave it to his secretary just to watch her drive off with his dream car and blow him the famous ex-employee good-bye kiss on Monday morning.

Isn't that the truth?

Ever been to Graceland?

Well, I'm originally from Canada. When I came to New York, I ran into a couple here that were telling me they went to Graceland. They were telling me, "Nita, it's not that far away, only about a day." This is really not a long drive compared to Canada. So I have my husband already primed. Next year, we're going to Graceland. Then we can go to our summer home for a week. So we'll do a week and a week. That's it. I said, "If that doesn't happen, we're not going anywhere!"

■ **TRIVIA ANSWER** / Answer to question on previous page

Scotty Moore

Daniel, I have to tell you something. I love Joe's new book. I can't tell you how much I loved it. It was absolutely amazing. The saddest part was the chapter when Elvis passed. Just reading all the different interviews of the people you had in the book and the things Joe said were so moving.

I was left with a great sadness and the pain everyone around him felt. No disrespect to this poor little girl Ginger Alden since she was just only a young girl. I have to believe that had Linda Thompson, Priscilla or Sheila Ryan been there, they would have checked on him sooner. They definitely would not have gone back to bed after the knock went unanswered. I think maybe he could have been saved if she would have been more persistent. So I feel such a great sadness when I read that chapter and see that unfold. I can't help but hang and shake my head and think, man, that's Elvis, the King of Rock 'n' Roll, the guy that did BLUE HAWAII and the ALOHA FROM HAWAII show. I can still hear the news reports vividly. Dead at 42, rock 'n' roll has died today. Even the funeral was surreal. I remember seeing the white limousines, the ocean of flowers, the teddy bears, and the guitars. God, even his departure from us was an incredible event. Wasn't it?

It sure was, Juanita. That is a very, very powerful and emotionally gripping chapter. Especially when you look at the images and the facial expressions of the people being interviewed. It will definitely pull on your heartstrings. It will hit you pretty hard.

■ **TRIVIA QUESTION** / View answer on next page

Which recording pioneer would do more to change the world than anyone in history?

Well, you get such a sense of how many people really loved him. Yet, you sense the loneliness. I said to my husband, "I think that was the strangest thing about Elvis, but it's something I can relate to." I have a huge family of brothers and sisters. It was only this morning, I was saying to my mom, "I come from a big family, yet, I feel like I'm alone." My husband doesn't get that. I feel the same thing so many times. My mom says, "I don't get it." When I read that in the book, I could totally see how Elvis felt.

That's just like when you hear Linda Thompson. You get that sense. Especially when she talks about when they were covering everything on the news. She says, "You can't go onto the next news story. There's nothing else. You know?"

Exactly! I was reading that and said, "Oh my god! I so see it. Oh my God. I so see that!" An event like that is not just a little news blip. This is Elvis Presley you're talking about! We grew up with him. He was so much a part of our lives. That's family you're talking about! There is just such a gigantic void since Elvis left that nobody, and I mean nobody, can fill, nobody.

That void felt like the world was hit by a nuke that took everything from us. The totality of the loss we experienced as Elvis fans is probably as profound as someone telling us that we just lost all of our friends and family members in one shot. We are all alone in the world now. The shock and stupefying enormity of someone like Elvis leaving was and still is inconceivable. Let's face it. We have yet to see an entertainer that comes close to having the same musical style, charisma and everything Elvis gave us as people.

■ **TRIVIA ANSWER** / Answer to question on previous page
Sam Phillips

When Elvis died, my mom and my brothers were watching it on the news and the movie specials that started coming on. It's so weird. It's like when President Kennedy got shot and died. It was such a void left in the world. I remember when Princess Diana died. Now it might not be as intense in the States as it was in Canada and in Europe, but a lot of people really loved her and got terribly affected by her death.

I remember what my dad was saying. I can still remember this as if he just said it yesterday. "Elvis has left and so has Princess Diana. We loved both of them, and they left us. You know these were people you took into your heart, so when they left a part of us died too." I just remember how tragic the death of Elvis was. Seeing the women sitting on the curb crying and being held by their crying daughters. My dad was crying and he never cried, never!

Let's face it. We all cried when Elvis passed away. You could have probably flooded the world with all of the tears that were shed during that time. Nobody was immune to his passing. You had people that never showed their emotions, pillars of society and giants of industry tearyeyed and weeping openly when all of that was happening.

Oh my God! My dad had tears rolling down his face like I do right now, Danny. They rolled over his cheeks. I was staring at him wide-eyed, the same with my mom. My dad was saying, "The world will never, ever be the same. The world will never be the same now that Elvis is gone." My dad is gone now too, but he was right.

■ **TRIVIA QUESTION** / View answer on next page

What was the address of the home Elvis stayed at while he was training in Fort Hood, Texas, in the Army and who was the owner of the house?

It's true. Elvis was and still is the ultimate gift mankind ever received. A happening that was just magical. When he passed he left us with messages in the form of his songs that we can apply to any situation in our life. Talk about a goodwill ambassador.

Absolutely!

Juanita, look at him in THAT'S THE WAY IT IS, seeing him with Joe on the back of the bike, clowning around in the recording studio during rehearsals. You see him on-stage interacting with the fans. You can see his reactions to their reactions. You see all of this unfold right in front of you. You can't help but love what this guy can do. I mean look at the breadth and depth of his talent. In my opinion, it's about as limitless as you can get.

Oh, Absolutely! It's the weirdest thing. I don't know. A lot of people I know, when I talk to them, like the younger Elvis. Well, everybody laughs at me because I liked Elvis as he got older. I like the older look. I liked him even when he had weight on because that's never been an issue for me, weight on a person.

It's called unconditional love

That's unconditional love. That's right.

You know it goes past looks. Elvis was a feeling, a presence, and a variety of different things to many people. You don't start judging a family member with statements like "My god boy! You should really lay off them chips before your drivers license reads photo continued on the other side." You accept them for the great human beings they are. You love them no matter what they look like.

Well, you know what? My husband put it best. I worry about him a lot since he has a couple of pounds on. He looks at me and says, "You know what? I am totally comfortable in my fatness and my baldness. You're the one with the weight worries in this house!" I just laugh. I tell this to our insurance guy who does our life insurance. He says, "Damn! I like your husband already because I'm a little fatling and sure could use a few pointers on how to stuff my wife's hole under her nose. She's always saying that I'm so fat and that I need a boomerang to put on my belt. She's always poking fun at me."

I look at my husband, and I love him no matter what. I said, "I love you fat. I like you bald. I like you driving a bus. It doesn't matter to me."

I love my guy, and that's how I look at Elvis. I can look at pictures on Joe's site. You might say that this is crazy but there are certain ones I look at when Elvis was older. I swear to God. I have chills running down my back. I would imagine standing in front of Elvis looking like that and not being able to have a conversation with him. I would stand there like a mute fool with eyes bugging out of my head! My husband said, "Nita, there is no power in the Universe that would make you mute!"

[Laughing]

■ **TRIVIA QUESTION** / View answer on next page

Who uttered the following words, "I wouldn't have him on my show at any price, he's not my cup of tea?"

As I look at Joe, and am looking at the different pictures on the site with different people he's met, it's almost like when Joe was here at the Elvis thing we have up here in Saratoga, up in the Lake George area. One year, Joe was the guest. Well, I almost fell off the sofa when I read that in the paper. I kept saying, "You've got to be kidding me! You've got to be kidding me." Joe finally comes here, and I have to be bound by a legal contract I have with the hospital. It says I have to work at least fifty weekends a year. I couldn't believe it. Of course, that weekend Joe was there, I was going crazy! I was so excited that he was here, but I never got to see him.

What would you tell Joe Esposito if he was on the telephone with you right now?

Oh God! I would thank him for being, obviously, such a great friend to Elvis Presley, a great manager on the road and a true man of integrity. Even in the pictures, you can see the integrity Joe has. When I hear him speak, I sense it in my soul. My husband always says that I'm a good judge of character. I would just like to thank him for giving his life to Elvis like that. I know that if Elvis could sit down and say something today, it would be to thank Joe. Joe's been and stayed his friend. I thank you for living your life while raising your family and being married. That's got to be horrible, trying to live your life like that, especially with the intense lifestyle surrounding Elvis. Loving your family, paying bills, like we all have to do, and still taking care of things for Elvis at the same time is tough. I am sure, he knew, he had

■ **TRIVIA ANSWER** / Answer to question on previous page
Ed Sullivan

found in you a person that really cared for him. Joe, thank you for being a great guy with a lot of heart and integrity. You kept your dignity while some of the others around Elvis have since disgraced themselves in a variety of different ways. Sure, we knew Elvis was taking prescription drugs. He did stuff to cope. Some people drink, others shoot people in the post office, beat a punching bag, or dig the dirt around in the yard. We all have to cope somehow in this life. Elvis coped the best he could. By comparison to some of the legendary rock stars, he not only stayed with us longer, but also handled himself exceptionally well publicly. Thank God for Joe! There's a special place for him in heaven with everything he's doing and all the people he has gathered around him, including you, Daniel. There has to be love there. TCB Joe is obviously not a nine to five outfit. It comes across as something that really has a lot of love and personal commitment in it, in order to do that. From me to Joe, "You did great!"

Thank you for all of your kind words. Juanita Pasquini from New York, Ladies and Gentlemen. ♦

Did You Know?

Dancer and actor, Gene Nelson, along with music director, Fred Karger, picked the music for KISSIN' COUSINS. ♦

■ **TRIVIA QUESTION** / View answer on next page

Which one of Elvis's co-stars would grow up to become the first lady of Hawaii?

What Really Happened?

Interview Excerpt with Joe Esposito

Reporter: Joe, there is a well-known picture showing Elvis at the helm of a boat during a Bahamas vacation. What do you remember about that?

Joe Esposito: I'd have to see that picture of the Bahamas vacation. He's driving a boat?

He's wearing a blue shirt and a captain's hat. You're sitting in front of him with a red shirt on, curled to one side, since you don't look too comfortable. He has a Hav-A-Tampa in his mouth.

Oh! That was a boat in Hawaii. That picture was taken in Hawaii about 5 or 6 months after Lisa Marie was born. We all took a vacation in Honolulu, Hawaii. We were staying at the Ilikai Hotel.

One day, while we were there, Elvis said, "Joe let's get a boat, go out and do some fishing." I said, "Ok." So I chartered this boat. We all took off and went out into the ocean. We didn't fish. We just had a good time boating around and just hanging out with our wives and each other. Some of the guys had their girlfriends with them. That's all it was, just a little boat ride.

So the Bahamas trip never existed?

Oh yeah! We went to the Bahamas but we didn't take a boat ride in the Bahamas.

■ **TRIVIA ANSWER** / Answer to question on previous page

Vicky Tiu Cayetano

Here's the story. We went to Paradise Island for a quick vacation and arrived at this nice hotel late at night. The very next morning, you hear all this wind blowing and howling. We looked out of the window and saw the palm trees bent all the way down to the sand on the beach! A huge, big hurricane hit that island and confined us to that hotel for about 3 days. We couldn't go out because of the dangerous wind. All we did in those 3 days was go to the casino and watch some of the production shows they had going on there. After a few days, the weather let up enough for us to go out a little bit. That's when we decided to go jet skiing. There were no jet skis in the United States at that time. They were just at Paradise Island. So we rented a bunch of jet skis. I have home movies that show Elvis riding a jet ski in the water, very cool. We also took speedboats, shot over to some of the other islands and hung out at the beaches there, but we never went on a big boat ride at all while we at the Bahamas.

So are the Bahamas the only place you guys ever rode the jet skis?

Yeah, actually it was. Elvis never owned a jet ski. ◆

Did You Know?

Sammy Davis Jr. saw Elvis and the guys off at the bus after Elvis completed the FRANK SINATRA WELCOME HOME ELVIS SPECIAL and were heading back to Memphis. ◆

■ **TRIVIA QUESTION** / View answer on next page

How much was Elvis paid for the three ED SULLIVAN SHOW appearances?

Always On My Mind

My name is Richard Stables. I live in Stonehaven in the northeast of Scotland. I've been an Elvis fan for as long as I can remember. I think that my earliest recollections are from me playing dad's collection of 45's. What got me hooked was watching Elvis perform on the ALOHA FROM HAWAII concert via satellite broadcast when it was first aired in the UK in 1973. I was instantly struck by Elvis's charisma and stage presence. That fact alone even amazes me to this day. I then began to spend my pocket money on records and magazines, anything related to Elvis. I have everything from records to compact discs to a large selection of photographs and books. I also have a few menus from Las Vegas and Lake Tahoe. My treasured Elvis possession is a Las Vegas Hilton room service menu signed by Elvis in his hotel suite in December 1975. I had hoped to one day travel and see Elvis perform live, but unfortunately my dreams were shattered when I heard of Elvis's death on August 16, 1977. I was only ten then, but I remember it vividly. I then began dreaming of visiting Graceland but didn't get the opportunity to go until 1997. My favorite memory of that trip is probably walking up the Graceland driveway in the early hours of the morning before the tours started and spending some quiet time at the meditation garden. It makes me sad thinking about that, when I think about Elvis. I should really be happy since he has given me so much over the years and he still does, everyday, just by listening to his music. Elvis has affected me very deeply. Even though I am only 38, and I kind of missed out on the most part of Elvis's life, he means so much to me and always will. ♦

■ **TRIVIA ANSWER** / Answer to question on previous page

$50,000

What Really Happened?

Interview Excerpt with Joe Esposito

Reporter: It is widely known that Elvis created and recorded at Graceland in the room that is now called the Jungle Room. What do you remember about this time and what do you think led to Elvis wanting to record at Graceland?

Joe Esposito: Well, Felton Jarvis came up with that idea. Felton was his producer and just felt that Elvis maybe wanted a different surrounding than just the regular studio in Nashville. He wanted to do something different. Elvis was getting tired of going into the recording studio in Nashville at that time. So Felton said, "Hey, why don't we record at Graceland? You know it's a good room." As you remember, the carpeting was all over the floor, the walls and the ceilings. So that's good for sound reasons. It was great recording in Elvis's house. Everybody was having a ball just kidding around. Elvis was doing a great job, considering that he wasn't feeling too well when we started that recording session. So basically, it was a very short session. It wasn't like normal recording sessions where we'd go up to Nashville for a week or something like that. I think the Graceland recording sessions lasted about three days, and that was it.

There was a stupid rumor that surfaced about this particular recording session. It basically said that Elvis and I were on top of the stairs and were both standing there, dressed in black suits and fedoras, like mob guys, shooting the room up with Thompson submachine guns because

---

■**TRIVIA QUESTION** / View answer on next page
On which TV show did *Heartbreak Hotel* make it's debut?

Elvis was fed up with everything and didn't want to record records anymore.

Yeah sure! How stupid is that fairy tale! Not only would the bullets have destroyed the house and caused multiple fires; but considering the small size of the room, the ricochets from the weapons we supposedly used most definitely would have killed everyone in that room including us! ♦

Up Close and Personal: Elvis and Steve McQueen

A candid conversation between Joe Esposito and Daniel Lombardy

Daniel: What did Elvis think about Steve McQueen, Lee Marvin and all those guys when they were coming out with those movies back then?

Joe: Elvis loved Steve McQueen. He thought he was a great actor. As we all know, Steve McQueen was a great actor who made great movies. Lee Marvin he also liked very much. I think he liked them because they were doing the type of movies he wanted to be making for himself. He really appreciated and admired the kind of movies they were making, tremendously. We would always view their newest movies in Memphis before the theater audience would get to see them. It was great. We saw Steve quite a few times at 20th Century Fox while we were making movies in Hollywood. We talked and hung out with him on occasion. Yes, Elvis was a fan of Steve McQueen, very much so. ♦

■ **TRIVIA ANSWER** / Answer to question on previous page
The DORSEY BROTHERS STAGE SHOW

Always On My Mind

My name is John Campolo. I live in Kenosha, Wisconsin. I've been an Elvis fan for over 40 years. I first got interested in 1956 when I saw Elvis on the ED SULLIVAN SHOW. I was about seven years old at the time. I didn't really get into Elvis until about 1968 when an old girlfriend pointed out the '68 COMEBACK SPECIAL to me. My thing for Elvis really took off from there. I've turned into a really big Elvis collector since. I collect records, pictures and everything associated with Elvis. He's really affected my life. I mean, he's my number one singer. All I listen to is Elvis music. I think his music will probably go on 'til the end of time. ◆

What Really Happened?

Interview Excerpt with Joe Esposito

Reporter: What did Elvis do with the cows after he bought the Circle G Ranch?

Joe Esposito: The Santa Gertrudis cows? They were just beautiful cows. They were gorgeous, not just typical cows. They had a great fur to them and were very beautiful looking. One of the conditions of the ranch sale was that they came with the ranch. So Elvis said, "Hey, this is their home. You've got to keep them here."

They weren't free-range cows. They had a certain area that was fenced off just for them. Yeah, he would go out and look at the cattle. It was just part of being a rancher. He did the ranch bit for about a year and a half. ◆

■ **TRIVIA QUESTION** / View answer on next page
In which Elvis movie did you hear Elvis sing only once?

Up Close and Personal:
The making of THIS IS ELVIS

A candid conversation between Joe Esposito and Daniel Lombardy

Daniel: During the making of the movie, you were a consultant. What feelings do you remember having being back at Graceland and reliving the past?

Joe: Well, I felt very good that Jerry and I were invited to be consultants for this movie project; especially working with experts like David Wolper, Andrew Solt and Malcolm Leo. We were very honored to be working with people that great. We knew that the end product of this project would be fantastic unlike other movies depicting the life of Elvis that you see today. I was told by a lot of fans and people that knew Elvis that this movie was the best ever about Elvis's life. This makes me very proud since I was so closely involved. There were times during shooting where it got very tough, especially when we were filming in his bedroom and his bathroom. That was a tough reminder of what happened. Jerry and I talked about this project a lot during and after filming. I do commend David, Malcolm and Andrew on doing such a fantastic job on the finished product.

You are right, Joe. I also commend you and Jerry for making sure that every detail and nuance about Elvis's life made it into the movie. It really came through how much both of you cared for Elvis and how important it was for everyone involved in the project to tell the story properly and with respect.

Thank you. ♦

■ **TRIVIA ANSWER** / Answer to question on previous page

CHARRO

What Really Happened?

Interview Excerpt with Joe Esposito

Reporter: Joe, what do you remember about the times Elvis met Isaac Hayes during recording sessions in Memphis?

Joe Esposito: You know, Elvis met a lot of different people he admired and respected while he was doing different recording sessions. I remember the great recording session we did in Memphis at American Recording Studios. Isaac Hayes was there. If I'm not mistaken, it was the time when Isaac was in a recording session. They asked him to leave. So Isaac says, "Why do I have to leave? I'm recording!" Then they told him that Elvis was coming in. At that he said, "Oh! ok, we'll leave." He was a great sport. So he met Elvis when he came in. Elvis loved Isaac Hayes. He loved the way he sang with that big deep powerful voice of his. They met and they talked for a while, and it was a great meeting. That's the way Isaac felt about Elvis. Elvis is coming in. It's his recording studio now. Elvis really appreciated him making room for him when he got there. Isaac is a very nice man and one of the best entertainers around. ♦

Did You Know?

Elvis presented a Ceremonial gift of two Tennessee hams from Tennessee governor, Buford Ellington, to Washington Governor, Albert Rosellini, on the final day of location shooting for IT HAPPENED AT THE WORLD'S FAIR. ♦

■ **TRIVIA QUESTION** / View answer on next page

Which Elvis co-star would later turn into a Genie?

Always On My Mind

I'm Linda Mackenzie, and I'm in Victoria, Australia. I have loved Elvis 45 years or more. His music picks me up when I'm down. Everything from his movies and his music is just so charismatic. He's so beautiful. It's impossible to not love him. You can't not love him. You just feel so good after listening to him. That's what he does to me. ♦

Did You Know?

Elvis was fitted with brown contact lenses for his role as a half-breed in the movie FLAMING STAR. ♦

Up Close and Personal: Elvis in Aspen

A candid conversation between Joe Esposito and Daniel Lombardy

Daniel: Do you still remember the times when Elvis, you and the guys were in Colorado riding the snowmobiles?

Joe: I sure do. We were, I believe, in Snowmass on that trip. I had rented a house for Elvis in this quaint little community that did not have a lot of houses, which was great. Actually, if I remember correctly, Priscilla went up there with me a month earlier to look around for a suitable house for us all to stay in. After awhile, we found one that was just great. So I rented it for a certain amount of time. So one day, we all went up there. Our party included Priscilla, Elvis, Lamar and his wife Nora, Charlie, Joanne and me.

■ **TRIVIA ANSWER** / Answer to question on previous page

Barbara Eden

I remember there were no TV sets or telephones around in that place so it was easy for us to actually just sit around and enjoy our own company without getting distracted or interrupted by calls and things like that. We would sit around and discuss life and everything. It was just great. I believe that only Vernon had the number to reach us in case of an emergency. The privacy we had at this place was just great. After a few days of unwinding, Elvis wanted to rent some snowmobiles since he was not a skier. Sure enough, we got hooked on those. Elvis loved them so much, he told me to look into buying some. So I called the snowmobile dealership to bring some down. Naturally, he took the best one. It was a Yamaha. This rocket was red and really fast. Our friend, Ron Pietrafeso in Denver, still has the red snowmobile Elvis gave him.

He was a police officer, right?

Yes, a police officer and a good friend of ours. He traveled with us quite a bit.

So here we are riding snowmobiles all over the place everyday. It was like the Beatles in the movie HELP. It was a lot of fun. Just imagine snowmobiles zigzagging all over the place, pretty hilarious. Boy was that fun. Poor Charlie missed out on all the fun since he came down with a cold and was really sick the entire time and confined to his bed. I felt so bad for him since we were out having the time of our lives on those little machines. Here he is laid up in bed sick.

■ **TRIVIA QUESTION** / View answer on next page
  What role did Charles Buchinsky play in Elvis's life?

We would often sit around in the evenings and have great conversations or play board games like Monopoly, Yatzee or different card games. This place really brought out the feeling of being in a tight knit family. It brought out a good warm feeling in you. I consider myself very fortunate to have been around at moments such as these, especially since these events meant so much to Elvis. I will always be thankful for that. ♦

Did You Know?

Elvis's pet chimp, Scatter, was on the set of GIRLS! GIRLS! GIRLS! wearing a Hawaiian shirt. ♦

Always On My Mind

My name is Maria Hesterberg. I'm from Germany and the city is Bonn, the former capital. Elvis affected my life by becoming a part of my life. So that he affected, yeah, mostly every part of my life because his music um… did so much to me. When I'm down and if anything goes wrong, I feel very inspired and feel much better after listening to him and um… yeah. He affected my whole life since I was eleven years old. Although my personality changed, the affection I have for Elvis and the passion I have for Elvis never changed. So I could go on for hours and hours of telling you more stories but I think that was the point, the main point. He was and is still, my steady companion in my life. ♦

■ **TRIVIA ANSWER** / Answer to question on previous page

Charles Buchinsky, also known as Charles Bronson, made a movie with Elvis called, KID GALAHAD.

What Really Happened?

Interview Excerpt with Joe Esposito

Reporter: Did Elvis meet any recording stars during his recording sessions?

Joe Esposito: Elvis met other stars during his recording sessions all the time. One of the stars Elvis met was Roy Hamilton. It did not matter what he came out with. Elvis loved the way Roy Hamilton sang. Elvis thought he was one of the greatest singers around. You have to remember, he sang great ballads too. He had a great warm voice. Elvis loved it. In fact, I have a picture of Elvis and Roy Hamilton. It's one of the few that were ever taken of both of them, and I put that in a couple of books I published before. ♦

Up Close and Personal: Snowmobiles and Powder

A candid conversation between Joe Esposito and Daniel Lombardy

Daniel: Tell me about the times you guys went out on the snowmobiles.

Joe: Well, since the house was located very close to the slopes, we would take the snowmobiles up the slopes at night, since they came equipped with lights. Let me tell you something. We were having a ball. We would shoot up and down the slopes. It was very cool.

■ **TRIVIA QUESTION** / View answer on next page

Prior to the '68 COMEBACK SPECIAL, when was the last time Elvis appeared in front of a live audience, and what was the occasion?

Eventually, the ski patrol caught us in the act one night and told us, "You know you can't do this stuff guys. We're out here for hours smoothing the slopes for the next day, and you're up here tearing up the powder!"

They were telling the truth. There were tracks everywhere! You could not find an inch of snow that was not trampled on or tore up by us. It was pretty funny. So we stopped doing that at night. So of course, we came up with something else in it's place. We discovered those snow dish type things that you sit on and fly down the slopes with. We would hike up the slopes and ride these dishes down without messing up the slopes at all. So that was a terrific discovery that did not upset the ski patrol guys.

I do remember one time, not sure if it was Billy Smith or not, anyway, most ski slopes have the telephone poles or something all up and down the mountain. Billy ran right into one of those head on. We thought for sure that he got killed when he hit. It was almost surreal watching that. He hit so hard. It was like watching those test car dummies smacking into the windshield after an impact. He lucked out that he didn't get seriously injured or anything.

That was a bad hit. Swishh…thwack hits the pole full force…and stays down. You see, once you got going with those things, you couldn't really control them. You sit in them and pray hard that you don't hit anything on the way down or fall out. Seeing that put an end to us playing around with those things. That's for sure. ♦

■ **TRIVIA ANSWER** / Answer to question on previous page
It was the 1961 benefit concert in Hawaii. It was put on to help fund the building of the U.S.S. Arizona Memorial at Pearl Harbor.

Fan Spotlight Interview

With Dawn Stedman

My name is Dawn Stedman, and I'm from Lawrenceville, Georgia. I had a friend who lived across the street from me who loved Elvis. He introduced me to Elvis, and then I just fell in love.

I hear that a lot. Tell me what are some of your favorite Elvis movies and Elvis songs?

I love BLUE HAWAII and JAILHOUSE ROCK.

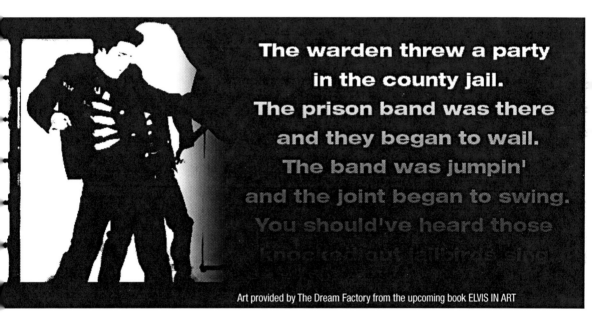

The warden threw a party in the county jail.
The prison band was there and they began to wail.
The band was jumpin'
and the joint began to swing.
You should've heard those
knocked out jailbirds sing.

Art provided by The Dream Factory from the upcoming book ELVIS IN ART

I don't think there is a bad song. I love every single song he sings.

Dawn, you have great taste.

Thank you.

■ **TRIVIA QUESTION** / View answer on next page
Which event is considered by many to be the ultimate showcase of Elvis Presley?

Tell me, If you had Joe Esposito on the phone with you right now what would you tell him?

Actually, I would ask him questions since I missed out on seeing Elvis perform live. I was only a little girl when he passed away. I would just love to know what he was like, just the person, not the entertainer on-stage, the person he was while sitting around the house, the person he was when he was away from the cameras. I cannot imagine how amazing an opportunity Joe had to know him as a friend. How cool that has got to be, having the memories Joe has of Elvis.

He has so many good memories, Dawn.

I'm sure he does, Daniel.

Is there anything you would like to say to the fans reading this right now?

I would like to let every Elvis fan know that we are very, very, special people. I believe that if we are to keep his memory alive, we all need to pull together as true Elvis fans. ◆

Always On My Mind

My name is Stephane Roussel. I'm a French native living in Holland. How Elvis influenced my life; I mean right now. Um, everyday I am listening to Elvis. According to your mood you can listen to rock 'n' roll or easy listening. In this way, Elvis can help you cope with some moment you can have in your life, good and bad. So this is how Elvis is walking with me at this point. ◆

■ **TRIVIA ANSWER** / Answer to question on previous page
The '68 COMEBACK SPECIAL

Ask Joe

I have a letter here from Jeff Aron.

Jeff says:

Hi Joe, can you tell me if Elvis ever saw any of the footage that was filmed for the 1977 CBS special? If So what was his reaction to it?

Elvis never got to see any of that special, ok? He was not in the mood to see it. I think that maybe he wasn't too happy with it, but he never made that known to anyone or said it. He never saw a lot of his own stuff, Jeff. Even when he was making movies, he never saw them. You know, he did see the dailies while they were working on the film. As far as actually seeing the completed films, he didn't care to see himself on the big screen. So to answer your question, Jeff, I cannot tell you what his reaction was to the special since he never saw it. ♦

What Really Happened?

Interview Excerpt with Joe Esposito

Reporter: Did Elvis ever meet Englebert Humperdinck?

Joe Esposito: Elvis did meet Englebert Humperdinck. Englebert appeared to be very shy and not too relaxed around Elvis. I cannot tell you if it was because of the typical affect Elvis had on people including stars or if Englebert, by nature, is a very shy person. Not sure. Elvis wanted to meet him because he was and still is a great singer to this day. ♦

■**TRIVIA QUESTION** / View answer on next page

What was the cost of making the ALOHA FROM HAWAII special?

Up Close and Personal:
The Dune Buggies

A candid conversation between Joe Esposito and Daniel Lombardy

Daniel: Tell me about Elvis and the dune buggies.

Joe: Palm Springs, that's where it all started. We used to hang out there quite a bit. So we were at Liberace's place. He lived near the house Elvis rented in Palm Springs. Since Elvis and Liberace were friends, we would often go to Lee's house to hang out, talk about show business and that sort of thing. So one time, Elvis and Lee were talking. He noticed that Lee had a beautiful black dune buggy. You have to remember dune buggies were really hot back then. So it caught Elvis's attention right away. He said, "I need to get me one of those." Lee said, "Well I'm thinking about selling this one." So Elvis told Lee that he would be interested in buying it. So that's exactly what he did. He bought the dune buggy from Liberace. It was really cool. It had a Volkswagen engine in it, and it was really pretty. That's what started the dune buggy phase. So one day, we are driving around Palm Springs, and Elvis notices a dune buggy at a dealership. It was a gorgeous metallic green, pretty little thing. We pull into the dealership to take a closer look at it, and Elvis asks me, "Joe, you like this dune buggy?" I said, "Yeah. It's very nice." "Why, hell, I'll buy it for you." So he bought it for me. My dune buggy was better than his because it came with a Porsche engine. It was really cool, man. So we used to go ride around on the sand dunes with chicks. I can still see him driving his, and I would be driving mine. It was like our own version of EASY RIDER. Man, we were It! Unforgettable!

■ **TRIVIA ANSWER** / Answer to question on previous page
  $2.5 million dollars

You had a pretty bad accident in your dune buggy one time. What happened?

Yes, that was a bad accident. It happened at night, and we were driving the dunes at night. Of course you're not supposed to for the reasons I am about to tell you. Anyway, we would jump these dunes after we drove around scouting for suitable dunes to jump over. So we would first drive around slowly, then drive back around and hit the dunes at full speed to make sure we got some good hang time. So I am looking at Elvis, and he's flying real good. I'm going real good. We are having a blast doing our version of Evel Knievel in this incredible display of fearlessness. Then, it happened. I miscalculated the number of dunes that were supposed to be coming up and plowed head first into a boulder! They tell you that you are supposed to be in a trance, part fuzzyheaded and disoriented when you get into an accident. With me, it seemed that I just skipped that part and just went right to the pain part. It was like Fred Flintstone high diving into a drained swimming pool, feet sticking up out of the tiles at the bottom of the pool and everything!

Let me tell you! Steering wheels and lips don't mix. I broke my tooth and was bleeding like a fifty year-old cook who lost control over his potato gun. Thank god, nothing happened to the young lady that was with me.

You had a lady in the buggy with you?

Yes, I did.

■ **TRIVIA QUESTION** / View answer on next page
What role did Marty Passetta play in Elvis's life?

I see. So what did she think of the night flight to Venus?

Oh, nothing really. She just said that no one was to blame for the crash. It never would have happened if I had been looking ahead instead of at her. ♦

What Really Happened?

Interview Excerpt with Joe Esposito

Reporter: Joe, since you were practically around Elvis all the time, what could you tell us about how Elvis prepared before he would go into the studio to rehearse or to record?

Joe Esposito: There was nothing special he would do. He didn't prepare for a recording session. He automatically knew what he had to do. He would bring stacks of demos to the studio that he wanted to record. Once at the studio, he would connect, shoot the breeze with all of the musicians and catch up on what they were up to in their lives, that sort of thing. After awhile, he would start playing some of the demos with direction as to what he was interested in doing and how he wanted to go about recording a particular piece. So there was no specific sequence or ritual like gargling with salt or getting into a trance before going into the recording studio. He didn't have to prep his voice or anything like that. He just went in there and recorded. That's the way it happened. That was just the way it was. ♦

■ **TRIVIA ANSWER** / Answer to question on previous page
He produced and directed the ALOHA FROM HAWAII special.

Always On My Mind

Hi, my name is Terry Muise. I'm forty-seven years old, and I'm from Nova Scotia, Canada. I remember being eight years old the first time I heard Elvis. Right from that moment, I loved the music. I remember there was a store, uptown, in the town I lived in, that had these shoes in the window. They were black with pointy toes and gold on the side. I used to tell my grandmother that I want a pair of them Elvis shoes. I always called them Elvis shoes.

As I got older, I kept listening to Elvis. Then things changed, and he started singing ballads and stuff. It really made me feel good. It was just amazing what that man did with his voice. That voice just touches you and makes you feel good inside. Now, all these years later, every single day when I go to work, I put my Elvis tape in and I listen to him. Every single day, when my job is done, I put my Elvis tape back in, and I listen to his music all the way home. I also do this when I'm driving on long trips or something. I bring all my Elvis stuff and keep listening to it. I have a picture of him in my truck. It was his last fare-well from his Indianapolis, Indiana, concert June 26, 1977. It's up here in my visor. Sometimes, I just listen to the music, look at him and still think that he's around although I never ever did meet the man. It just feels like I've known him since I was a little kid. What he's done and what he's still doing is just amazing! I'll be listening to him until the end of time. ♦

■ **TRIVIA QUESTION** / View answer on next page
Who introduced Elvis to Ann-Margret and vice versa?

Did You Know?

"Flaming Lance" was used as the pre-production title before evolving into "Black Star" and would eventually be released as FLAMING STAR. ♦

What Really Happened?

Interview Excerpt with Joe Esposito

Reporter: We know that Elvis recorded "U.S. Male" by Jerry Reed, but did Elvis ever have the opportunity to play music together with Jerry?

Joe Esposito: I have a story about Jerry Reed you might find interesting. Felton Jarvis once hired Jerry Reed to come and play guitar because his regular guitar player was not available. Jerry, at the time, was at the brink of becoming popular. Jerry just came in and was thrilled to death to meet Elvis Presley. He was such a fabulous guitar player. Elvis really enjoyed the hell out of the tunes he created with his guitar. As we all know, he eventually became red hot and took off like a rocket. That was a fun session. Let me tell you. There was a lot of singing and a lot of carrying on. Some of those guitar licks Jerry Reed came up with were amazing. What a fantastic guitar player. ♦

Did You Know?

Elvis was at McKellan Lake at Riverside Park in Memphis when his father married Dee Stanley. ♦

■ **TRIVIA ANSWER** / Answer to question on previous page

Director, George Sidney

Up Close and Personal:
An Unusual Request

A candid conversation between Joe Esposito and Daniel Lombardy

Daniel: I heard that Elvis was very demanding at times. Can you remember anything that really sticks out?

Joe: Well, one of the funniest ones, and I have told this story many times, is when Elvis was dating Sheila Ryan. She later would go on to marry actor James Caan. So he was dating her, and we were on tour somewhere on the East Coast, Baltimore, I believe. Elvis says, "Joe, call Sheila and have her join us on tour." I said, "I'll call and see if she's available." He said, "Naw. You can get her here. Don't worry about it."

So I call Sheila up and she says, "Joe, I can't come. I have a screening for a part in a movie tomorrow. I have to be here for this." I said, "We'll have to come up with a really, really good excuse. I'll just tell him that you're sick, that your nose is running and your ears are infected, really bad."

Joe, you're killing me here. I think I just cracked my back from laughing so hard!

You ok, buddy? You sound like an elephant just sat down on your chest. Anyways, I call the ear, nose and throat doctor to at least let him in on what he needs to be saying for his part. He said, "No problem, Joe. Don't worry about it."

So Elvis wakes up and asks, "Did you get a hold of Sheila?"

I said, "Yeah, I got a hold of her but she can't come."

■ **TRIVIA QUESTION** / View answer on next page

Who said the following words, "Elvis did the best white Ray Charles I've ever heard?"

He says, "What do you mean she can't come?" I said, "She has a really bad ear infection and a cold. The doctor recommends that she does not fly because the altitude is not good for her ears." So he says, "Oh, come on! She can come. Get her on a train."

I said, "A train? We're only here for one night! She won't be able to get here before we leave." So he says, "Damn it! Charter a plane! Tell the pilot to fly really low."

I said, "Elvis! You can't just fly low. You have to be up there!" ♦

Always On My Mind

My name is Eric Murray. I'm from Toms River, New Jersey. I'm 41 years old. All I do since his death is listen to his music 24/7. His music just calms me and makes me feel so much better when I listen to him sing. I just got the satellite radio service, and it's on all the time. The way Elvis lived his life impacted me because he came from nothing to become what he was and still remained a gentleman. His generosity, his patience and performance on stage are everything, the whole package. I mean, he had It! There is nothing this man could not do that wouldn't impress me. So I mean, he was just…he was just the greatest. ♦

Did You Know?

Elvis owned a 16-foot, powder blue, water-skiing boat. ♦

■ **TRIVIA ANSWER** / Answer to question on previous page

Sammy Davis Jr.

Always On My Mind

Hi, my name is Dianna Weisner, and I live in Rockville, Maryland. From the time I was nine and heard Elvis singing *Heartbreak Hotel*, he has always been on my mind. Ahh, I love his music. I don't think there's a song that I don't like. I mean people will say this is my favorite or that's my favorite, but I can't even pick a favorite. I really, really can't because down through the years from 1956 'til now, they're still playing his music, and they're all great. I'll tell you, I've lived long enough to hear lots of entertainers down over the years through Disco to whatever. Above all, I really love Elvis, and I will forever. If I'm feeling sad, blue or lonely, I put Elvis on, and I just listen to him sing. It just makes me feel a whole lot better. Just knowing about Elvis and who he was, not just the songs, how much he loved life and how much he loved his fans had an affect on people. It really had a big affect on me. He was just a great human being and a wonderful entertainer. I absolutely love him. I don't know what else to say. He's just been the best and will always live on in the hearts of his fans. ♦

Did You Know?

Columnist, Vernon Scott's, remark about Elvis's upcoming enlistment into the Army was, "Could not be any worse than the merry-go-round he's been on for the past two years." ♦

■ **TRIVIA QUESTION** / View answer on next page

What were some of the food specialties found on the menus during the Elvis Presley Day celebration on September 26, 1956?

What Really Happened?

Interview Excerpt with Joe Esposito

Reporter: During IT HAPPENED AT THE WORLD'S FAIR, you see Kurt Russell kicking Elvis in the shin. Who came up with the idea to put that into the film?

Joe Esposito: The director came up with that idea. Remember, Elvis in the movie was trying to come up with an excuse to see the nurse. So he was trying to figure out a way to go meet this nurse that he really liked a lot. So he gave this little boy I think $5 or $10 to kick him in the shin. That happened to be Kurt Russell. That was his first little bit in a movie. That's who it was. That's when Elvis came limping into the hospital saying, "I got hurt. I hurt my knee." That was the director's idea.

What else do you remember about Kurt Russell being on the set?

Nothing really. It was only a one-day job when you think about it. It wasn't like he was there everyday for a few days. It was just one day. That was it. So we didn't really get a chance to spend anytime with him. Since there were so many people at the fair, most actors would usually go back to their trailers to rest and prepare for their next scenes. Can you imagine a big star like Elvis between takes hanging out and chewing the fat in the middle of all those people? Some of those women were aggressive! Quite frankly, I think he would have caused a stampede that would have left most of the entourage with claw marks, bites, bruises and nibbles. ♦

■ **TRIVIA ANSWER** / Answer to question on previous page
Love Me Tender steak, *Ready Teddy* pork chops, *Hound Dog* and *Heartbreak Hotel* cobbler.

Up Close and Personal:
James Brown

A candid conversation between Joe Esposito and Daniel Lombardy

Daniel: What do you remember about Elvis and James Brown?

Joe: Elvis was a big fan of James Brown because James was and still is a great soul singer. When you saw James perform on-stage, you could see that he sang from the heart. Elvis loved the way he moved on-stage. They met several times on different occasions. They were sort of friends. They did not hang out together, but Elvis really appreciated this gentleman as a person and as an entertainer. James Brown appreciated Elvis the same way. So whenever we were in Vegas, James would come to see the show, and we would go see his. As you know, when Elvis passed away, James flew in the night of the first viewing of Elvis. He came to pay his respects to Elvis and his family, especially Vernon. James was very, very emotional that Elvis had left us at such an early age. ♦

Did You Know?

Elvis sent his parents a telegraph that read, "Hi babies. Here's the money to pay the bills. Don't tell no one how much I sent. I will send more next week. There is a card in the mail. Love, Elvis." ♦

■ **TRIVIA QUESTION** / View answer on next page

How long did the band called, The Tennessee Two, tour with Elvis, and who was their lead singer?

Always On My Mind

My name is David Cammack and I'm from Manteca, California. Elvis affects my life everyday. I find that listening to Elvis can be a therapy or get the blood pumping depending on my mood. I would challenge anyone to listen to songs like *Anyway You Want Me, Fame & Fortune, The Thrill of Your Love, I Gotta Know,* or *Lawdy Miss Clawdy* and not be in a good mood after would be a good sign your from another planet or on life support. My love for Elvis has extended to our 15 year-old granddaughter, Ashley, who now likes Elvis a lot. ◆

What Really Happened?

Interview Excerpt with Joe Esposito

Reporter: It was said that Elvis had an incredibly hectic schedule when he started playing in Las Vegas. How many shows would Elvis generally do during his engagements in Las Vegas?

Joe Esposito: We signed a contract to play the International Hotel. It was for two times a year. Usually, it was in January and August. We would play twenty-eight days, two shows a night. That's fifty-six shows. That's what we did, two shows a night. Eight o'clock and twelve o'clock, non-stop, no days off, not like today. You just did it; and we did that for about five years. As time went on, we noticed that a lot of other shows were cutting back the number of shows they were doing. I mean, Frank Sinatra cut back to one show a night. In fact, he called

Elvis at the hotel one time, and they put the call through to me. Of course I am surprised that Frank Sinatra was calling. He says, "This is Frank." And I recognized his voice right away and I said, "Yes, Mr. Sinatra, what can I do for you?" He said, "Well, do me a favor," he says, "I know Elvis is asleep now, but tell him we should start changing things around here in Las Vegas. Just do only one show a night. It's too hard to do two shows a night, seven days a week." And I said, "Well, I'll relay the message." I told Elvis about the call and this is what he said. Elvis said, "No problem with me. I like doing two shows a night." But eventually, as we all know it all changed and became one show a night. It's tough. Vegas is a very tough city to sing in, especially because you get what singers call Vegas throat. What it means is that the dryness of the desert would dry up your throat and you couldn't sing. Most of the singers got Vegas throat one time or another.

Is that why Elvis started drinking a lot of Gatorade?

Joe Esposito: Elvis drank water more than Gatorade. He drank a lot of water all the time. The throat doctors always advised him with, "Drink a lot of water. Keep your throat moist, otherwise, ya know, you'll lose you voice." ♦

Did You Know?

Red Foxx attended Elvis's Wedding? ♦

■ **TRIVIA QUESTION** / View answer on next page
What car did Elvis, Scotty Moore, and Bill Black drive around in before they got the Cadillac Limousine?

Always On My Mind

My name is Shirley Toffling, and I am from Albuquerque, New Mexico.

I can from the time I was born remember loving Elvis. It started with a song called, *I Got Stung*. I think my little feet just started moving by themselves and they haven't stopped since. I miss him terribly and play his music all the time. ♦

What Really Happened?

Interview Excerpt with Joe Esposito

Reporter: It was once said that Elvis pulled a prank on Jimmy Dean while he was onstage. What happened?

Joe Esposito: Yes, that did happen. Elvis in Vegas, when we went around different shows, different places, ya know, he was a character, Elvis. He did what he wanted, the impulse thing. I remember one time we watched Jimmy Dean with Jimmy Ellis, a big fan of Jimmy Dean's. During the show, we noticed that Jimmy Dean's microphone was starting to go bad, and he was obviously having problems with it. So Elvis went back stage and walked out on stage and gave Jimmy a new microphone, like a sound guy. So of course Jimmy was shocked. I mean he just couldn't believe that Elvis was walking out and giving him the microphone. But Elvis did those things all the time. He was great. I remember one time he got on stage with Don Rickles, and Don didn't know what to do. It destroyed Don's act. He didn't know how to react.

■ **TRIVIA ANSWER** / Answer to question on previous page
A 1954 Chevy Bel Air

Elvis just went up there and talked to Don a little bit. And Elvis got off stage and Don said, "Boy that sure screwed up my act."

Were you there when Elvis and the rest of the guys walked across the stage at the Bill Medley show?

Joe Esposito: Well, Bill Medley was playing the lounge at the International Hotel. Elvis would watch all the acts at different times in the lounge; Kenny Rogers and The First Edition, Ike and Tina Turner. Great acts. They were there the same time we were playing in the hotel. Elvis would go see these guys all the time. They didn't even know it half the time. He'd go in the back after the show started and watch the show. We'd all see it and then leave, and they would come see Elvis's shows. Well, Bill became a good friend. Bill, I would say, is one of the nicest guys in the business. So Elvis one time, he says, "Okay, let's go over and give Bill a shock." He'd say, "Let's go see Bill's show. We'll walk across the stage and not say a word. I'm gonna walk ahead. You guys all walk behind me." We walked right across the stage while Bill's singing. And that's what happened. Bill is out there singing, ya know, one of these big songs, and all of a sudden people are just shocked. He didn't know what was going on because he didn't see us. All of a sudden, he turns to pay attention, and Elvis was walking by. "How ya' doin' Bill?" Walked right by, we all walked by. Bill didn't know what to do. He didn't know how to act, and it was great. Bill says, "Oh well," and he starts singing again. And Elvis did it again. He walked back the other way on stage. He did it a few times with Bill, ya know, just to break the monotony. ♦

■ **TRIVIA QUESTION** / View answer on next page
What was the name of one of Elvis's favorite blues men who at one point became a contract farm laborer, and wrote the song that would cause Elvis to go into the recording studio in the first place?

What Really Happened?

Interview Excerpt with Joe Esposito

Reporter: We have heard that the Colonel at one point drew up a contract with Alex Shoofy on a white tablecloth. What led to this?

Joe Esposito: Well, Alex Shoofy first met with the Colonel about this deal on the contract. They were sitting in a coffee shop or something at the Flamingo, and during the meeting they wrote the contract out on a tablecloth with the Colonel. They wrote the contract and put all the points the Colonel wanted covered. That was the original contract. I never saw the contract. I was told that's what happened. I can't say for sure. I wasn't there. ♦

Always On My Mind

My name is Luke Mayama, and I reside in Lihu'e, Hawaii.

Seeing Elvis perform in Hawaii is what started it for me. I've since collected every movie, record and everything. I've turned most of my friends on to Elvis over the years, and I visit Graceland from time to time. I often sit and look at the ocean and listen to Elvis singing in the background wondering what would have happened to him and his music if he were still with us today. I guess that's one question we will never have answered but one thing is for sure, there's no denying what he did while he was still walking among us. ♦

■ **TRIVIA ANSWER** / Answer to question on previous page
  Arthur Crudup, the song *That's All Right Mamma*

Up Close and Personal: Gambling with Elvis

A candid conversation between Joe Esposito and Daniel Lombardy

Daniel: Did you and Elvis ever go out and gamble at the International?

Joe: Well, we did play a little bit. I liked to play blackjack and I like to gamble, which is a big mistake when you play Las Vegas. Elvis played a little bit, but not a lot. Maybe twenty dollars a hand. We'd go down late at night if we had nothing to do or just go down to have a good time and get out of the hotel room. But he never dealt cards. There was a story that Elvis dealt. Elvis couldn't even shuffle, much less deal. He was not a card player by any means. But, we'd go there, we'd take up a whole table and sit there and play. Jimmy Newman, the casino boss, was really nice. About four or five o'clock in the morning, when it was really quiet in the casino, he gave us a lesson about blackjack. He said, "Okay guys," he calls the dealer, "Let me deal the guys." So we're all sittin' there, Elvis is sittin' there and Jimmy says, "Okay I'm gonna' deal." He dealt all the cards to us. We all made our bets, and he turned both of his cards up. The dealer had both cards. You saw what the dealer had. And he said, "I'm gonna' teach you guys a lesson. So, ya know, if he turns over eighteen and you have twelve or seventeen, you have a hit. Naturally, you have to stick with seventeen. He's got you beat on top," he just said. Then he'd hit and you'd bust out. He just proved one thing, he says, "Ya know when you're hot, you're hot. Strategies only work up to a certain point," he said, "But it proves

■ **TRIVIA QUESTION** / View answer on next page
Who was the singer that entertained Elvis and a small group of soldiers during a special Christmas party in Germany in 1959?

one thing that a dealer eventually can't lose." Sometimes the player just can't lose. That's just how it goes. We all lost even though we knew the dealer's cards. So, that was just a little point about gambling. Either you're lucky at the time or your not. ♦

Always On My Mind

My name is Henry Lee from Pusan, Korea.

Elvis to me is a magical experience. You can put one of his songs on the record player and be transported back to a time where the world was different. I was in the hospital when it was announced that Elvis had died. I can remember crying so much they eventually had to call in a psychologist to calm me down. I like other fans took it pretty bad. Two of the songs that remind me of that time were *Moody Blue* and *Way Down.* I still choke up when I hear those songs because they remind me of that sad time. At the same time, I smile because he left us with such a rich body of work. Thank you, Elvis, for everything. I will never forget you. ♦

Did You Know?

The day before Elvis was to receive his first guitar for his eleventh birthday from his parents, he and his mother, Gladys, had to hide in a storm cellar when a tornado ripped through Tupelo. ♦

■ **TRIVIA ANSWER** / Answer to question on previous page
Charlie Hodge

Always On My Mind

My name is Frank Valente from Montreal, Canada.

I know that when I feel down, I put an Elvis album on and I forget about my problems. His songs are like a cure to sadness or a difficult time like a divorce that I went through. ♦

Always On My Mind

My name is Danielle Cantrell, and I am from Mississippi.

For as long as I can remember, Elvis has been a part of my life. My mother was an Elvis fan, and I fell in love with not only him as a person but also with his music. Elvis means so much to me. It is just amazing what his music does to my soul and my spirit. ALL OF HIS MUSIC. Elvis has helped me through some very rough times, and as always, he lifts my spirits. No one can sing gospel music like Elvis! Even though this is not my entire Elvis story, I just wanted everyone to know who is not already aware...Elvis is THE GREATEST entertainer/singer/celebrity/person (besides Jesus) that ever walked this earth! This world was very fortunate to have had Elvis in it. I wish that I could have known him personally. I was born one year, four months, and 13 days after the day he died. LONG LIVE ELVIS!!!!!!!!!! ♦

■ **TRIVIA QUESTION** / View answer on next page
What song resulted from Elvis's artistic and incisive amalgamation of *Dixie, The Battle Hymn Of The Republic,* and *All My Trials?*

Always On My Mind

My name is Steve, and I am from Australia.

I have been an Elvis fan since I was six. I'm 28 now and still a fan. His voice is amazing. I love to sit back and listen to the albums and watch all the movies and documentaries. From the stories I hear about his life, I could imagine how much of a fun, loving, cool and caring guy he was. I think he was a gift from God. ♦

Always On My Mind

My name is Danielle Offord, and I reside in the United Kingdom.

I'm only 16, and I am gutted that I wasn't alive when Elvis was. I truly love Elvis. I have been to Graceland. What an experience!! That's where my obsession started, and I am glad I got to go because now I have a better outlook on life. ♦

Always On My Mind

My name is Fay Freeman from Delaware, Maryland.

I was fortunate enough to see Elvis in concert in 1976. It was the experience of a lifetime. He will never be forgotten. Thank you Joe for all you do to keep his memory alive. We love you, too. ♦

■ **TRIVIA ANSWER** / Answer to question on previous page
American Trilogy

Always On My Mind

My name is Wendy Bishop, and I am from Durham, California.

How do you describe the effects of a tidal wave? How do you adequately appreciate a worldwide cultural phenomenon? Well, don't even try – just listen. Listen to his music then listen to your heart – it will be clear. He slips away from us, leaving behind a rare, beautiful fragrance that although we can't see, affects us, surrounds us, gets our attention. None of the ingredients are completely clear but together make something unique that is intriguing and we can't let go. We may try forever to dissect what made him Elvis, but he'll slip away again. That's what magic is. ♦

Always On My Mind

My name is Stephen Skrypnyk from Manitoba.

I've been a fan since I saw the '68 COMEBACK SPECIAL and thought, hmm, this guy has a great voice! But, that's not the only thing that made me a fan. Everything Elvis represented is to be celebrated. He never forgot where he came from, and regardless of where his concerts and movies took him, he always returned home to Graceland. No matter what daily life may hold for me, I always return to his music to soothe me. ♦

■ **TRIVIA QUESTION** / View answer on next page
Which Hank Cochran song does Elvis sing in the movie THAT'S THE WAY IT IS?

Always On My Mind

My name is Karlos Alvarez. Elvis is and will always be the greatest person who walked the earth. I have been a fan for over 30 years. Long Live The King. ♦

Always On My Mind

My name is Yvonne Smith from Nashville, Tennessee, and I have been an Elvis fan since 1967 when I received my first Elvis album for my 7th birthday. My Mom had always been a fan, and she and I began visiting Graceland every year. I saw Elvis in concert for the first time in 1972 in Nashville. It changed my life. I became SO Elvis obsessed that I decorated my entire room including the ceiling with Elvis. I saw many concerts after that and got a towel and a rose. In 1974 we were visiting Graceland, and as we passed by at night we saw a crowd there and the gates open. I was 14 and stepped inside the gates. I met Harold at the guard house and became friendly. We actually SAW Elvis that night as he returned from the Memphian Theater. My mom called my dad and said we would be staying in Memphis for the summer as long as Elvis was home...and we did that EVERY year after that. I have a thousand wonderful stories and met SO many wonderful people. Elvis called me jailbait whenever he saw me. I saw Elvis over 250 times, and I was president of Steamroller Dreamers EPFC. It had 6000 members worldwide. I was 15 when I started it. I appreciate

■ **TRIVIA ANSWER** / Answer to question on previous page
  Make The World Go Away

Harold, Vester and Lloyd and all the Memphis Mafia guys that treated me, a teenager, so nice! You guys made every visit fun, and I love you all and miss the times we had together! I have returned to Graceland only a couple of times since the day I walked through to view Elvis's body, and it is NEVER going to be the same for me. I was there the night he passed and all through the funeral, and when I visit I remember how he teased me at the gates by giving me McDonalds coupons and how Vester would let me take mail to the kitchen and how Harold snuck us into the bathroom. I miss seeing Al drive out and fans following him, and then us catching up with Elvis at the Memphian. I miss Charlie's happy face and sweet nature and the doughnuts he shared on late nights. But, mostly, I miss the friendships that were made and the feeling of being one of Elvis group. Love to all of you guys that helped a young girl's fantasies come true! ♦

What Really Happened?

Interview Excerpt with Joe Esposito

Reporter: Mr. Esposito, I have just watched some footage on the Internet that showed you and Charlie Hodge in an interview with Geraldo in which you stated that you found Elvis in the bedroom instead of the bathroom as you said in later interviews. What do you have to say about this?

Read Joe Esposito's answer to t*his questio*n and many others in Volume 2 of the *Celebrate Elvis* series.

■ **TRIVIA QUESTION** / View answer on next page

When and where were the songs you can hear in the 1978 album release of *Forever Young, Forever Beautiful* originally recorded?

Two NEW releases *from Joe Esposito that compliment each other...and the legendary career of ELVIS PRESLEY!*

Long-time Elvis insider and right hand man, Joe Esposito, lends his invaluable insights and memories to not one but TWO exciting new series entries that will set you up and set you straight!

CELEBRATE ELVIS is just that... a celebration of Elvis's career, his life and his legacy. Loaded with fun stories, interviews, trivia and contributions from you, the fans.

CELEBRATE ELVIS is an uplifting, feel-good book that enlightens, entertains and informs!

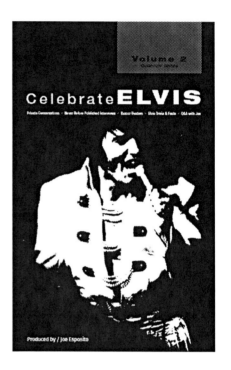

Available at:
www.celebrateelvis.com

NOT SOLD IN STORES

This item is part of our affiliate program. Please visit www.tcbjoepublishing.com to participate.

■ **TRIVIA ANSWER** / Answer to question on previous page
July, 1958, at Eddie Fadals house in Texas.

For the first time ever...**ELVIS-STRAIGHT UP!**

Joe Esposito and Joe Russo

Includes never before seen photos

Destined to become the most examined and talked about book since ELVIS, WHAT HAPPENED?.

NO MATTER WHAT YOU HAVE EVER READ BEFORE...

ELVIS-STRAIGHT UP! WILL CHANGE THE WAY YOU LOOK AT ELVIS PRESLEY.

**What was the "real" Elvis like?
The search for the truth is over!**

www.elvisstraightup.com

Available at:
www.elvisstraightup.com

NOT SOLD IN STORES

This item is part of our affiliate program. Please visit www.steamrollerpublishing.com to participate.

■**TRIVIA QUESTION** / View answer in volume 2

How much did Elvis make an hour when he first started driving a truck for Crown Electric?

Also Available

Remember Elvis
Produced by Joe Esposito

REMEMBER ELVIS is an all-encompassing, in-depth look at the life and career of a man whose popularity is unrivalled in the history of show business and who continues to attract millions of new fans each year.

This ground-breaking book is brimming with rare interviews, insights and experiences, previously unrevealed... until now.

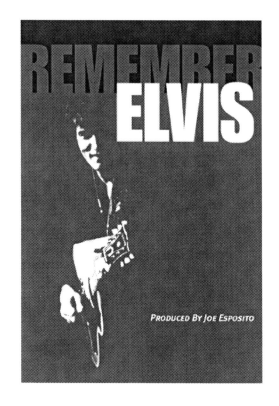

At the heart of this landmark project are over 200 interviews with many of Presley's most intimate associates, as well as some of the biggest names in the film and recording industries.

Available at:
www.rememberelvis.ca
and other fine online bookstores

This item is part of our affiliate program. Please visit www.tcbjoepublishing.com to participate.

Printed in the United States
82438LV00001B/165-186

9 780977 894536